Simple Computer Transfer and Backup

Simple Computer Transfer and Backup

Don't Lose Your Music and Photos

CA

with Eric Geier and Jim Geier

Wiley Publishing, Inc.

Simple Computer Transfer and Backup: Don't Lose Your Music and Photos

Published by
Wiley Publishing, Inc.
10475 Crosspoint Boulevard
Indianapolis, IN 46256
www.wiley.com

Copyright © 2007 by Wiley Publishing, Inc., Indianapolis, Indiana

Published simultaneously in Canada

ISBN: 978-0-470-06853-3

Manufactured in the United States of America

10 9 8 7 6 5 4 3 2 1

1B/QU/QR/QX/IN

For general information on our other products and services or to obtain technical support, please contact our Customer Care Department within the U.S. at (800) 762-2974, outside the U.S. at (317) 572-3993 or fax (317) 572-4002.

Library of Congress Cataloging-in-Publication Data
Geier, Eric, 1984-
  Simple computer transfer and backup : don't lose your music and photos / CA, with Eric Geier and Jim Geier.
    p. cm.
  ISBN-13: 978-0-470-06853-3 (paper/cd-rom)
  ISBN-10: 0-470-06853-1 (paper/cd-rom)
  1. Electronic data processing—Backup processing alternatives. 2. Data recovery (Computer science) 3. Multimedia systems. I. Geier, James T. II. Title.
  QA76.9.B32G45 2007
  005.8'6—dc22
                      2006101138

Credits

Executive Editor
Carol Long

Senior Development Editor
Tom Dinse

Production Editor
Felicia Robinson

Copy Editor
Kim Cofer

Editorial Manager
Mary Beth Wakefield

Production Manager
Tim Tate

Vice President and Executive Group Publisher
Richard Swadley

Vice President and Executive Publisher
Joseph B. Wikert

Project Coordinator
Jennifer Theriot

Graphics and Production Specialists
Brooke Graczyk
Denny Hager
Jennifer Mayberry
Erin Zeltner

Quality Control Technicians
John Greenough
Robert Springer

Proofreading
Techbooks

Indexing
Estalita Slivoskey

Anniversary Logo Design
Richard Pacifico

Acknowledgments

CA would like to thank all of the people who have contributed their technical, editorial, administrative, and/or creative expertise to the making of its first series of CA Simple computer solution books.

Laural Gentry

Diana Gruhn

Lawrence Guerin

Mark Haswell

Robyn Herbert

Christopher Hickey

George Kafkarkou

David Luft

Gary McGuire

Stefana Ribaudo-Muller

Contents

Part II: Transferring, Backing Up, and Restoring Your PC 15

Chapter 10: Connecting to the Internet   113

Chapter 11: Planning a Wireless Network Installation 131

Introduction

As you get more involved with PCs, you'll start accumulating tons of files, such as pictures, movies, and documents. In addition, you'll eventually have numerous software applications installed on your computer for work and pleasure. The proper periodic backup of your valuable data is crucial to ensure that you have it forever.

This book explains how to use CA Desktop DNA Migrator to effectively backup your data and migrate it to a new computer. As bonus material, this book also includes loads of information that will help you better use and expand the capabilities of your computer.

How This Book Is Organized

This book is organized in a very simple manner and is summed up by the following:

- First you can learn about the problems.
- Then you can learn about the solutions to combat those problems.
- Next you'll prepare to implement the solutions.
- Then the book will help you properly employ the solutions with step-by-step directions, illustrations, and tips.

Part I: Understanding the Issues and Solutions

The chapters in this part will help you understand the issues relating to the transfer and backup of your PC's files and settings. In addition, you'll be introduced to solutions that address these issues, which allow a seamless and simple migration of your PC's DNA to a new computer or a backup of your PC to safeguard your important information.

This part of the book is a good place to start before actually installing and using the included software, CA Desktop DNA Migrator.

Chapter 1: Like humans, computers are all unique. Just as our DNA defines our differences, so does a computer's DNA. Each person modifies or uses their PC to fit their needs, jobs, and personalities, making each PC's DNA unique. This chapter defines the data you should keep backed up and the issues related to manual backup procedures.

Chapter 2: Don't waste time relearning the way your new PC works. This chapter shows you how to complete an industry standard data migration with just a few clicks of a mouse and save hours of time by letting CA Desktop DNA Migrator do the work for you.

Part II: Transferring, Backing Up, and Restoring Your PC

This part of the book gives you step-by-step instructions on how to migrate, back up, and restore your PC's files and settings—also known as your computer's DNA—using CA Desktop DNA Migrator. This software addresses the many issues of performing manual transfers and backups, as discussed in Part 1 of this book.

This part of the book walks you through the installation of CA Desktop DNA Migrator and how to use the software in order to migrate, back up, and restore your PC's DNA.

Chapter 3: This chapter shows you how to install CA Desktop DNA Migrator, which is the first step toward quickly and easily safeguarding your documents and settings and transferring them to another PC.

Chapter 4: This chapter guides you through the process of transferring your music, photos, and other data using CA Desktop DNA Migrator.

Chapter 5: This chapter guides you through the process of backing up your music, photos, and other data using CA Desktop DNA Migrator.

Chapter 6: If your PC crashes or you run into other unexpected issues, such as finding out that a week ago you deleted an important file from your PC, and you have been backing up your PC with CA Desktop DNA Migrator, you're in luck—this chapter explains how to you can easily restore your saved files, settings, and other important information!

Chapter 7: This chapter shows you how to keep CA Desktop DNA Migrator up-to-date with any fixes or new features, which may include the migration and backup support of more system and application settings.

Chapter 8: This chapter discusses common problems and fixes you may experience when using CA Desktop DNA Migrator and also lets you know where you can get more help.

Part III: Bonus Material

The chapters in this part contain additional tips when you are dealing with a newer PC, which is likely your situation as you are using CA Desktop DNA Migrator. For example, included in this part of the book are bonus chapters that cover many applications such as those that may come preinstalled and topics such as wireless networking that you may be concerned or involved with after getting a new PC.

These bonus chapters save you lots of money by avoiding the need to purchase separate books on these topics. We just want to be sure that you get the best out of your PC!

Chapter 9: After you've completed a migration to a new computer there are still a few things you should address, such as how to dispose of your old PC and what you can do to keep your new PC running smooth.

Chapter 10: In the blink of an eye, the Internet—also referred to as the "web"—has gone from novelty to necessity, ingraining itself in our culture to such an extent that people don't just use it—they depend on it. This chapter gives you essential tips on how to connect to the Internet.

Chapter 11: Before embarking on the installation of a wireless network, you should do your homework by thinking about what you need and the issues you might run into. Get off on the right foot by looking through this chapter and answering your initial questions before plopping down money on equipment.

Chapter 12: The purchase, installation, and configuration of your new wireless network can take several hours. Before investing all of that time (and money), read through this general overview of the steps involved in this chapter.

Chapter 13: This chapter guides you through the process of installing a wireless card that enables your computer to "talk" to a wireless router.

Who Should Read This Book

Anyone who uses the Internet, email, or a computer should read this book.

Whether you are a self-proclaimed computer illiterate or a lifelong IT professional, this book will give you the tools and understanding to properly migrate and back up your valuable data, as well as make better use of your PC.

What's on the CD-ROM

This book comes bundled with a CD containing CA Desktop DNA Migrator, developed by Computer Associates (CA).

This software allows you to easily transfer and back up your unique PC DNA to your new, upgraded, or restored PC. For example:

- Data files and folders
- System and application settings
- Network and printer settings
- Email address books

By transferring your PC DNA from your old PC to your new PC, you will be up and running quickly, taking advantage of your new PC's features and functions while still enjoying the familiar desktop environment settings, data, and connections of your old PC!

Simple Computer Transfer and Backup

PART I

UNDERSTANDING THE ISSUES AND SOLUTIONS

In This Part

Chapter 1: Dealing with Your PC's DNA

Chapter 2: Understanding CA Desktop DNA Migrator

The chapters in this part will help you understand the issues relating to the transfer and backup of your PC's files and settings. In addition, you'll be introduced to solutions that address these issues, which allow a seamless and simple migration of your PC's DNA to a new computer or a backup of your PC to safeguard your important information.

This part of the book is a good place to start before actually installing and using the included software, CA Desktop DNA Migrator. You'll have a much better idea of why you need to back up and effectively transfer your files, and the introduction to solutions will smooth out the process of managing your PC's DNA.

1

DEALING WITH
YOUR PC'S DNA

Like humans, computers are all unique. Just as our DNA defines our differences, so does a computer's "DNA." By modifying or even simply using your PC as suits your needs, job, and personality, you make your PC's DNA unique.

What Makes Up Your PC's DNA?

Your computer's DNA consists of settings and files such as:

- System and application settings, things like your dial-up and network settings, and your time zone

- Desktop settings, such as background, mouse, screen saver, and taskbar

- Custom templates or macros used in applications such as Microsoft Word or Excel

- Address books

- Web page bookmarks and favorites

- Data files and folders like My Documents, My Music, or My Pictures

Issues with Performing Manual PC Upgrades

Getting a new PC or upgrading your existing one is great! What is not so great is trying to manually move your PC's DNA to the new or upgraded PC without the help of an application—as discussed later in this book.

Without your old PC's DNA, you will spend hours, maybe days, relearning how to set up the numerous settings and preferences on your new PC.

However, if you choose not to use a DNA or file transfer application, such as discussed later in this book, when moving to a new or upgraded PC you'll run into many problems, such as:

- **Wasted Time**

  Locating and transferring your files and documents to your new or upgraded PC will likely take much more time when done manually. After you've scoured through and gathered all your files and documents, you'll have to somehow get them to your PC. With the manual method, this means burning the data on countless CDs and then loading them onto the new or upgraded PC.

- **Lost Productivity**

  As discussed, you'll likely spend a great deal of time manually transferring your files and documents, so you might be without a PC, or at least certain applications, for some period of time. This can prevent you from getting work done, paying bills with your computer, accessing personal files and documents, and more until the transfer has been completed.

- **Missing Settings and Files**

  Very few users have the time or knowledge to locate all the files and settings that comprise a PC's DNA, which can account for much more than your personal files, documents, and applications. Remember your PC's DNA is also comprised of system settings and preferences, such your desktop icons, printer and network settings, folder preferences, and more.

  It is extremely difficult to manually match the settings and preferences (or PC DNA) of a new or upgraded PC to the computing environment that you are accustomed to on your old PC. The manual method might also actually result in mistakes and system errors, resulting in more time and money spent trying to fix the problems.

Performing Backups Is Essential

In order to preserve your PC's DNA and protect your personal files and documents, you should perform periodic backups of your PC. Receiving malware, such as viruses and spyware, can infect and destroy files, settings, and programs. You may even experience a system crash, destroying all the data. Therefore, you should be prepared by having recent backups of your PC's DNA and your files and documents, just in case the unexpected happens.

Issues with Performing Manual Backups

If you don't use a streamlined back-up application, as discussed later in this book, and you try to manually back up your computer, you'll encounter many issues, such as:

- **Wasted Time**

  If you manually back up your computer, it will take a great deal of time. You will have to think of all the settings, files, and information you want to back up. Then, you have to go to each application or folder and find out how to properly back up that particular data.

  For example, most address book applications, such as Microsoft Outlook, allow you to export the information; however, it will likely take time to learn how to do it and how to import the information if needed later.

- **Missing Settings and Files**

  You'll likely forget about many settings and files when manually backing up your PC. In addition, it may be impossible to manually save, export, or back up some settings and preferences of your PC.

  For example, it isn't really possible to save or back up settings, such as for printer and network settings, and icons and shortcuts on your Windows desktop and taskbar.

2

UNDERSTANDING CA DESKTOP DNA MIGRATOR

Don't waste time relearning the way your new PC works—complete an industry standard migration with just a few clicks of a mouse and save hours by letting CA Desktop DNA Migrator do the work for you.

General Information

CA Desktop DNA Migrator (see Figure 2-1), developed by CA, formerly known as Computer Associates, quickly and easily transfers and backs up your unique PC DNA to your new, upgraded, or restored PC. Included in this process are the following:

- Data files and folders
- System and application settings
- Network and printer settings
- Email address books

Figure 2-1: CA Desktop DNA Migrator product box

By transferring your DNA from your old PC to your new PC, you will be up and running quickly. You can take advantage of your new PC's features and functions while still enjoying the familiar desktop environment settings, data, and connections of your old PC!

With CA Desktop DNA Migrator, you can also back up your PC DNA on a recurring basis, allowing you to easily restore your DNA after a disaster event, such as a virus or system crash.

Why Choose CA Desktop DNA Migrator?

There are many reasons why you should choose CA Desktop DNA Migrator for PC transferring and backup needs:

- **Developed by a Trusted Company**

  CA provides software to 98% of Fortune 500 companies — which are among the world's largest — and to millions of home users worldwide.

- **Award Winning**

  CA Desktop DNA Migrator, formerly Desktop DNA, earned the PC Magazine "Editors Choice" award two years running for its ease of use and powerful, flexible functionality.

- **Smart Design**

    CA's desktop DNA technology was the first to market and is the U.S. patent holder for migration technology.

- **Powerful Technology**

    CA Desktop DNA Migrator supports more system and application settings than any other migration product on the market.

CA Desktop DNA Migrator Features

With powerful migration features, flexible user options, and extensive backup capabilities, CA Desktop DNA Migrator allows you to manage a migration that will meet your unique needs.

Flexible Migration Methods

Flexibility is critical to supporting migrations. For this reason, CA Desktop DNA Migrator was the first migration tool to offer two major system migration methods. Figure 2-2 shows where you indicate which method you want to go with.

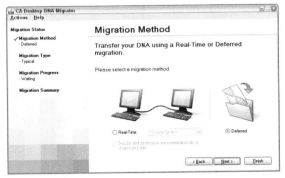

Figure 2-2: Choosing the method of your migration

- **Real-Time Migration**

    A Real-Time migration quickly streams your DNA information directly from your old PC to your new PC, which requires one of the following:

    - Both PCs are on a wireless or wired network and are able to communicate, or share files, with each other.

- A direct connection of the PCs using an Ethernet crossover cable plugged into the network cards, or adapters, of each PC.

- **Deferred Migration**

   A Deferred migration creates a DNA file containing your unique PC's DNA, so you can manually move the DNA file to the new PC, which requires one of the following:

   - CD or DVD burner, or writer.

   - Both PCs on a wireless or wired network and able to communicate or share files with each other.

   - Another method in which to transfer large files, such as with a flash or thumb drive.

Once the DNA file is transferred to the new or upgraded PC, you can simply double-click the file to apply your DNA from the old PC.

- **Performing Backups**

To use CA Desktop DNA Migrator to perform backups of your PC, in case of a system crash, you should use the Deferred migration method. Just backing up your PC doesn't necessarily require any transferring of information or the DNA file, as was discussed in the two previous situations.

After a system crash, or when a restoration is needed, you can simply double-click the DNA file to apply the saved DNA.

Migration Type

CA Desktop DNA Migrator offers two different migration types, discussed here and depicted in Figure 2-3, allowing you to choose the type that best meets your unique migration needs.

- **Typical Migration**

   A Typical migration takes the guesswork out of migrations by predefining the most common system and application settings, files, and folders to be collected and transferred. With a few clicks of your mouse, you can perform a complete migration.

   You can refer to the Appendix to see exactly what is transferred in a Typical migration.

- **Custom Migration**

    A Custom migration takes power, control, and flexibility even further by giving you the options to customize the settings and data you wish to migrate for your special migration needs.

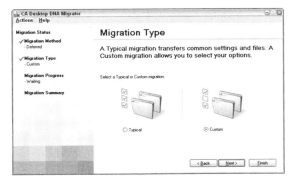

Figure 2-3: Choosing the migration type

Cross-Operating System and Application Migration

The settings you have customized on your old PC and in the older versions of your applications will seamlessly migrate to the new version of the operating system and applications. This time-saving feature will prevent you from trying to figure out where to set your customizations in the new locations, saving you time and effort.

Self-Extracting Files

If you select to perform a Deferred migration, a self-extracting DNA file will be created, allowing you to transfer the DNA file to your new PC over a network or burned to CD-ROM or DVD. Once the DNA file is on your new PC, simply double-click the file and the migration will take place, automatically transferring your DNA to your new PC.

Migration Progress

Never lose your place! The Migration Status on the left side of the screen, as shown in Figure 2-4, always lets you know where you are in your migration process.

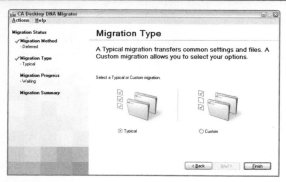

Figure 2-4: Migration status

Summary Screens

A comprehensive logging feature tracks the success of the migration and monitors the overall progress of the migration process. From the Summary screen, as shown in Figure 2-5, you are able to tell if there were any errors in your migration.

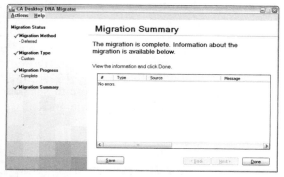

Figure 2-5: Summary screen

Undo File

An Undo file is automatically created and placed on your desktop, as shown in Figure 2-6, for both a Deferred and a Real-Time migration. This file allows you to return your PC to its pre-migration state with a simple double-click.

Figure 2-6: Desktop icon of the Undo file

Frequently Asked Questions

The following sections discuss many frequently asked questions about CA Desktop DNA Migrator.

What do I need to make the connection between my PCs?

You can transfer the DNA file with removable media, such as burning a CD, or via a network connection, either direct with an Ethernet cable or via a wireless or wired network.

For network transfers, CA Desktop DNA Migrator uses the TCP/IP network protocol to communicate between the systems. For a network migration, both systems need to have TCP/IP configured with CA Desktop DNA Migrator running. Don't worry, this is most likely installed, configured, and running by default on your PC. The CA Desktop DNA Migrator Wizard will automatically find other systems on the network and guide you through the process.

Does my PC need to be networked to use CA Desktop DNA Migrator?

No. You can transfer the DNA file with removable media, such as burning a CD.

Do I have to migrate everything?

No. CA Desktop DNA Migrator allows you the flexibility to select only the settings that you want to migrate. You can make an exact duplicate of your desktop or completely redefine your workspace to suit your individual workflow.

Does CA Desktop DNA Migrator migrate all of my application settings?

Currently, CA Desktop DNA Migrator moves the most commonly used application settings, such as settings from MS Office, Netscape Navigator, Excel, PC Anywhere, and *e*Trust(r) Antivirus or Norton AntiVirus. Periodically new applications and settings are added to the supported list; therefore, make sure you keep your software up-to-date.

You can refer to Appendix A for a list of supported application and system settings.

What settings does CA Desktop DNA Migrator migrate?

CA Desktop DNA Migrator migrates Windows OS settings including network addresses, printers, wallpaper, shortcuts, appearance, and so on, and personalized application settings including bookmarks, custom dictionaries, address books, toolbars, macros, signatures, and more.

The complete list of supported application and system settings are available in the following locations:

You can refer to the Appendix for a list of supported application and system settings.

Can I migrate application settings from one version of Windows to another?

Yes. CA Desktop DNA Migrator allows you to move your system and application settings from one Windows operating system (OS) or one version of an application to a newer version. For example, CA Desktop DNA Migrator can migrate the applications from a Windows 98 PC to one running a newer Windows, which is Windows XP. Keep in mind that if you are migrating applications, they must be compatible with both OSes.

PART II

TRANSFERRING, BACKING UP, AND RESTORING YOUR PC

In This Part

This part shows step-by-step how to migrate, backup, and restore your PC's files and settings, also known as your computer's DNA, using CA Desktop DNA Migrator. This software addresses the many issues of performing manual transfers and backups, as was discussed in Part 1 of this book.

This part of the book walks you through the installation of CA Desktop DNA Migrator and how to use the software in order to migrate, backup, and restore your PC's DNA. In addition, you'll be shown how to keep the software up-to-date, so you can take advantage of any new features. You are also provided with common problems and fixes so you can quickly resolve any issues that arise.

3

INSTALLING CA DESKTOP DNA MIGRATOR

Installing CA Desktop DNA Migrator is the first step toward quickly and easily safeguarding your documents and settings and transferring them to another PC.

System Requirements

The following requirements must be met, or exceeded, for the installation of CA Desktop DNA Migrator:

- 200 MHz Pentium processor or higher
- Windows 95, 98, NT 4.0, 2000, ME, or XP operating systems
- Internet Explorer 4.01 or higher
- 24MB RAM
- 20MB of hard drive space (more will be needed to perform a migration to the hard drive)
- CD-ROM drive

Choose Your Migration Method

Before beginning the installation of CA Desktop DNA Migrator, you should choose the migration method so you understand where you should install the software.

Real-Time Migration

A Real-Time migration quickly streams your DNA information directly from your old PC to your new PC, which requires one of the following:

- Both PCs on a wireless or wired network and able to communicate, or share files, with each other.
- A direct connection of the PCs using an Ethernet cable plugged into the network cards, or adapters, of each PC.

For this migration type, using either of these methods, you need to install the CA Desktop DNA Migrator software on both PCs.

Deferred Migration (or for Performing Backups)

A Deferred migration creates a DNA file containing your unique PC's DNA, so you can manually move the DNA file to the new PC, which requires one of the following:

- CD or DVD burner/writer.
- Both PCs on a wireless or wired network and able to communicate, or share files, with each other.
- Another method in which to transfer large files, such as with a flash or thumb drive.

For this migration type, using these methods, you only need to install the CA Desktop DNA Migrator software on the source (or old) PC, or the PC you would like to back up.

Installing CA Desktop DNA Migrator

To install CA Desktop DNA Migrator, which is included with this book, follow these steps.

Step 1

Insert your CA Desktop DNA Migrator installation CD into your drive. The installation will begin automatically.

If your installation fails to start automatically, you can launch it by browsing to the drive containing the CD and double-clicking the setup.exe file in the Setup directory.

Note

If you are installing the software specifically to perform a migration, make sure you install the software on the source PC (your old PC).

Step 2

You should now see the Choose Setup Language dialog box, as Figure 3-1 shows.

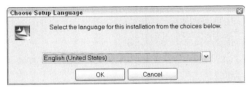

Figure 3-1: Choose Setup Language dialog box

Select a language from the drop-down list and click OK.

Step 3

After the installation wizard has finished loading you should see the dialog box shown in Figure 3-2.

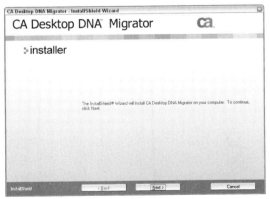

Figure 3-2: CA Desktop DNA Migrator Installation Wizard

To continue, click Next.

Step 4

On the next screen, shown in Figure 3-3, you will be prompted to accept the license agreement.

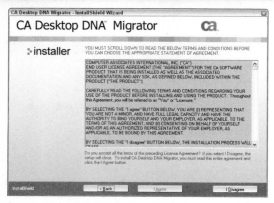

Figure 3-3: CA Desktop DNA Migrator license agreement

If you agree with the terms of the license agreement, click the I Agree button.

If you disagree with the license terms, click the I Disagree button and the installation will not continue.

Tip
For the I Agree button to work you may have to scroll through the entire agreement.

Step 5

This screen as shown in Figure 3-4 prompts you for user information.

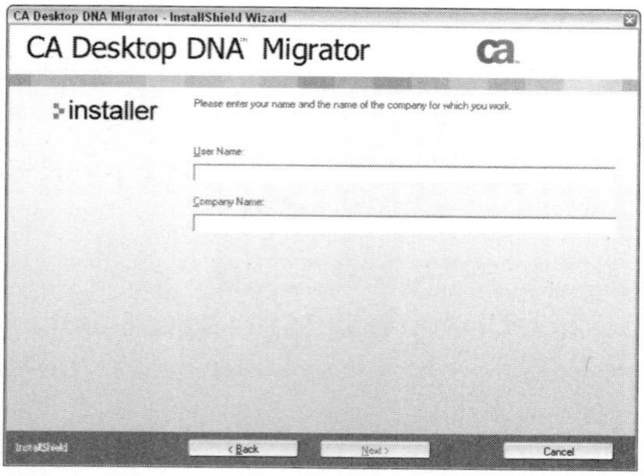

Figure 3-4: CA Desktop DNA Migrator User Information dialog box

Type your name and company, or organization, into the respective fields, and then click Next.

Tip
If you aren't installing the software for use in a business or organization, you could input your name in the field instead.

Step 6

You should now see the Installation Location dialog box, as seen in Figure 3-5.

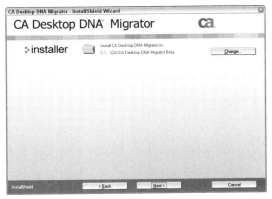

Figure 3-5: Installation Location dialog box

The default installation folder is "C:\Program Files\CA\CA Desktop DNA Migrator."

The default setting should be fine. If so, click Next to continue.

If you wish to select a different folder, click the Browse button, find another location, and click OK. Then click Next when you're done.

Step 7

You should now see a screen such as shown in Figure 3-6.

Figure 3-6: Install dialog box

To proceed with the installation, click Install.

Step 8

After the completion of the installation, you should see the final screen, as seen in Figure 3-7.

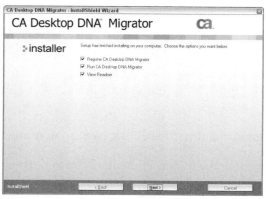

Figure 3-7: Installation Completed dialog box

Mark the checkboxes as desired, and click Next to continue.

Note

In order to register you must have a connection to the Internet.

Step 9

You should now see the InstallShield Wizard Complete dialog box, as seen in Figure 3-8.

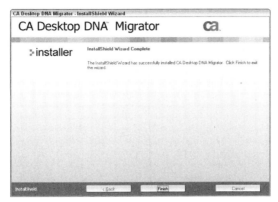

Figure 3-8: InstallShield Wizard Complete dialog box

To finish the entire installation and to exit the wizard, click Finish.

You're Done!

Congratulations! CA Desktop DNA Migrator is now installed on your PC.

4

MIGRATING YOUR DNA TO A NEW PC

This chapter guides you through the process of transferring your music, photos, settings, and other data using CA Desktop DNA Migrator.

Your Migration Options

CA Desktop DNA Migrator offers two different methods, as well as two different migration types, which are discussed in the following sections, for transferring or backing up your settings and data.

Migration Method: Real-Time or Deferred?

You need to choose which method you would like to use for your migration, by referring to the descriptions and requirements listed here:

- **Real-Time Migration**

    A Real-Time migration quickly streams your DNA information directly from your old PC to your new PC, as depicted in Figure 4-1, which requires one of the following:

    - Both PCs on a wireless or wired network and able to communicate, or share files, with each other.

    - A direct connection of the PCs using an Ethernet crossover cable plugged into the network cards, or adapters, of each PC.

Figure 4-1: Example of a Real-Time migration

- **Deferred Migration**

    A Deferred migration, as illustrated in Figure 4-2, creates a DNA file containing your unique PC's DNA, so you can manually move the DNA file to the new PC, which requires one of the following:

    - CD or DVD burner, or writer.

    - Both PCs on a wireless or wired network and able to communicate, or share files, with each other.

    - Another method in which to transfer large files, such as with a flash or thumb drive.

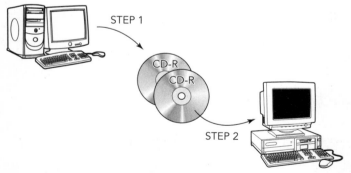

Figure 4-2: Example of a Deferred migration

Once you transfer the DNA file to the new or upgraded PC, you can simply double-click the file to apply your DNA from the old PC as discussed later in this chapter.

Migration Type: Typical or Custom?

CA Desktop DNA Migrator offers two different migration types, discussed here and depicted in Figure 4-3, allowing you to choose the type that best meets your unique migration needs.

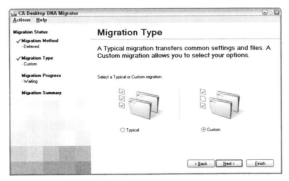

Figure 4-3: Choosing the migration type

- **Typical Migration**

    A Typical migration takes the guesswork out of migrations by predefining the most common system and application settings, files, and folders to be collected and transferred. With a few clicks of your mouse you can perform a complete migration.

- **Custom Migration**

    A Custom migration lets you take control over your migration by giving you the options to customize the settings and data you wish to migrate for your special migration needs.

Performing a Real-Time Migration

The following are the steps — discussed in detail in the following sections — for performing a migration using the Real-Time method:

Step 1:   Get Ready

Step 2:   Connect the PCs

Step 3:   Set up DNA Migrator on the Old PC

Step 4:   Set up DNA Migrator on the New PC

Step 5:   Complete the Migration

Step 1: Get Ready

Prepare for the migration by completing these tasks:

- **Install the Software on Both PCs**

  Because you're going to transfer your files using the Real-Time method, you need to install CA Desktop DNA Migrator on both PCs. (Refer to Chapter 3 if you need information about the installation.)

- **Disable Firewall Protection on Both PCs**

  To ensure CA Desktop DNA Migrator will be able to work properly, you should disable any active firewall protection on both PCs.

  The following steps show you how to disable Windows XP's firewall utility:

  1. Open the Control Panel, as shown in Figure 4-4.

Figure 4-4: Opening the Control Panel

Note

If the Start menu is in classic mode, the Control Panel is under Settings on the menu.

  2. Click Network and Internet Connections if the Control Panel is in category view, as Figure 4-5 shows.

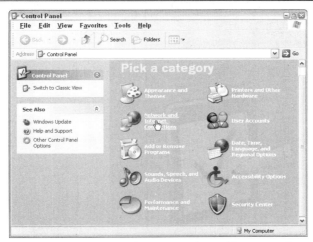

Figure 4-5: Opening the Network and Internet Connections category

3. Click Windows Firewall, as shown in Figure 4-6.

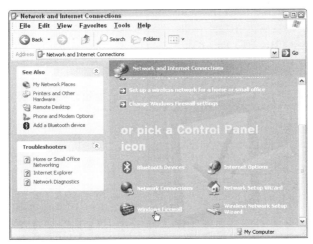

Figure 4-6: Opening the Windows Firewall options

4. Go to the Advanced tab.

5. In the Network Connection Settings section ensure the firewall protection isn't enabled for the particular network connection you'll be using for the migration by making sure its entry is unchecked, as Figure 4.7 points out.

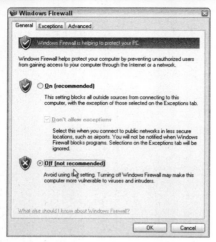

Figure 4-7: Ensuring firewall protection is disabled

Note

Be sure to reset the firewall setting on your new PC after your migration is complete.

- **Get Your Old PC Ready**

  Before starting the migration you need to do the following on your old PC:

  - **Log in with administrative privileges**

    Ensure your old PC is logged on a Windows account with administrative privileges.

    If you are not sure about this, you can check in this way:

    1. Open the Control Panel, as seen in Figure 4-8.

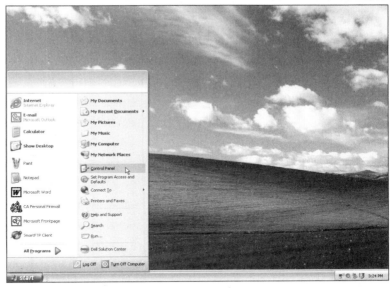

Figure 4-8: Opening the Control Panel

Note

If the Start menu is in classic mode, the Control Panel is under Settings on the menu.

2. Open User Accounts. (Figure 4-9 shows this when Control Panel is in category view.)

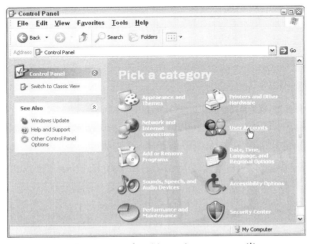

Figure 4-9: Opening the User Account utility

3. Look for your user account and see if it belongs to the administrators group, as identified in Figure 4-10.

Figure 4-10: Checking for administrative privileges

- **Run anti-virus and anti-spyware scans**

  This ensures that you are not migrating any viruses or spyware to your new machine.

- **Exit all programs on your old PC**

  Disable any anti-virus or anti-spyware protection and close all applications on your old PC, because they could interfere with the migration process.

Step 2: Connect the PCs

Because you are performing a Real-Time migration, your PCs must be connected during the entire process by one of the two methods discussed in this step.

Using an Ethernet Crossover Cable

If you are using an Ethernet crossover cable to connect your old and new PCs, connect the cable to the two PCs now.

Using Your Network

If you are using a common network to connect the two systems, ensure both the PCs are connected to the same network.

When using a wireless (or Wi-Fi) network, you can quickly check what network you're connected to by hovering over the system tray icon, as shown in Figure 4-11.

Wireless Network Connection (linksys-g)
Speed: 54.0 Mbps
Signal Strength: Excellent
Status: Connected
3:31 PM

Figure 4-11: Checking your wireless connection

Step 3: Set up CA Desktop DNA Migrator on the Old PC

You need to set up the software on your old PC by following these steps:

1. Open CA Desktop DNA Migrator, which can be accessed by browsing to the following path on your Start menu:

Programs (or All Programs) → CA → CA Desktop DNA Migrator

Then click CA Desktop DNA Migrator, as shown in Figure 4-12.

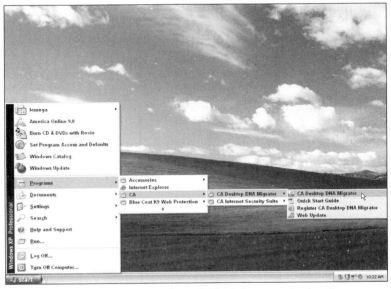

Figure 4-12: Opening CA Desktop DNA Migrator via the Start menu

2. The Welcome screen should appear, as Figure 4-13 shows. Click Next.

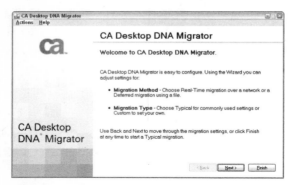

Figure 4-13: Welcome screen

3. Select the Real-Time migration method, as shown in Figure 4-14.

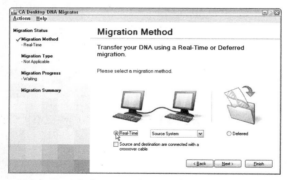

Figure 4-14: Selecting the Real-Time migration method

4. Select Source System from the drop-down list, as Figure 4-15 shows.

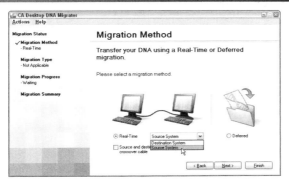

Figure 4-15: Choosing the Source System option

If you are using an Ethernet crossover cable to connect your two PCs, mark the applicable checkbox.

Click Next.

5. You can enter a password to protect your settings and data. This is optional and is recommended only if you are connecting the two systems over a network.

6. Click Finish.

CA Desktop DNA Migrator then waits for the new PC to connect.

Step 4: Set up CA Desktop DNA Migrator on the New PC

You need to set up the software on your new PC by following these steps:

1. Open CA Desktop DNA Migrator, which can be accessed by browsing to the following path on your Start menu:

Programs (or All Programs) → CA → CA Desktop DNA Migrator

Then click CA Desktop DNA Migrator, as shown in Figure 4-16.

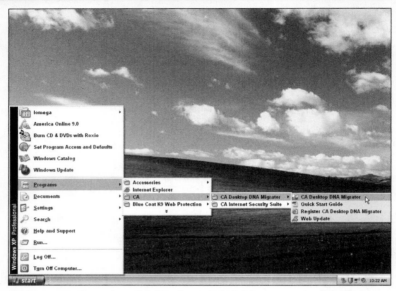

Figure 4-16: Opening CA Desktop DNA Migrator via the Start menu

2. The Welcome screen appears, as Figure 4-17 shows. Click Next to begin.

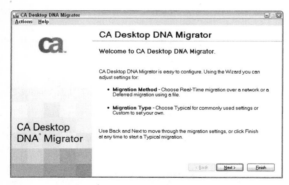

Figure 4-17: Welcome screen

3. Select the Real-Time migration method, as shown in Figure 4-18.

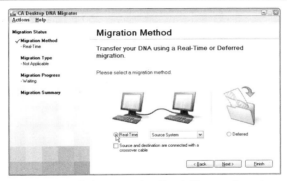

Figure 4-18: Selecting the Real-Time migration method

4. Select Destination System from the drop-down list, as Figure 4-19 shows.

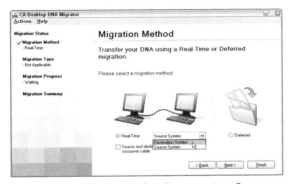

Figure 4-19: Choosing the Destination System option

If you are using an Ethernet crossover cable to connect your two PCs, mark the applicable checkbox.

Click Next.

Step 5: Complete the Migration

Follow these steps in order to complete the migration:

1. Select the old PC from the list, as Figure 4-20 shows.

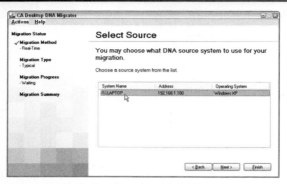

Figure 4-20: Selecting the old PC

Keep in mind that it may take a few moments for the PC to appear in the list.

2. If you do not want to customize what will be migrated, click Finish (and enter your password if prompted) to start the migration, otherwise follow these steps to customize what will be migrated:

   a. Click Next.

   If a password was specified on the old PC, you are prompted to enter the password.

   b. Choose a Migration Type and continue with the following steps:

   Typical

   This automatically selects common items to be migrated. Simply click Finish to start the migration.

   Custom

   Allows the option of selecting or clearing items to be included in the migration. Click Next. In the Custom Migration window, click Edit next to any category to make changes. Then click Finish to start the migration.

3. When the migration is complete, the Migration Summary window, shown in Figure 4-21, displays the information about your migration.

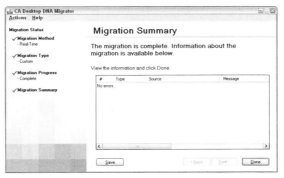

Figure 4-21: The Migration Summary window

Click Done to exit CA Desktop DNA Migrator.

4. You are prompted to restart your new PC after the migration is complete.

Click Restart. All migrated settings may not be available until you restart the PC.

Note
During the migration an Undo DNA file is automatically created on the desktop. This file may be used to undo the settings and data applied during the migration and return the PC back to the pre-migration state. To undo a migration simply double-click the Undo file on the desktop.

Congratulations, you have successfully completed your migration using CA Desktop DNA Migrator!

Performing a Deferred Migration

The following are the steps, which the next sections discuss in detail, to perform a migration using the Deferred method:

Step 1: Get Ready

Step 2: Start the Migration

Step 3: Move the DNA

Step 4: Complete the Migration

Step 1: Get Ready

Prepare for the migration by completing these tasks on your source (or old) PC:

- **Install the Software**

  Because you are using the Deferred migration method, you only need to install CA Desktop DNA Migrator on the source PC. You can refer to Chapter 3 for more information on the installation.

- **Run Anti-virus and Anti-spyware Scans**

  This ensures that you are not migrating any viruses or spyware to your new machine.

- **Exit All Programs**

  Disable any anti-virus or anti-spyware protection and close all applications on your old PC, because they could interfere with the migration process.

Step 2: Start the Migration

You can start the migration process by creating your DNA file:

1. Open CA Desktop DNA Migrator, which can be accessed by browsing to the following path on your Start menu:

   Programs (or All Programs) → CA → CA Desktop DNA Migrator

   Then click CA Desktop DNA Migrator, as shown in Figure 4-22.

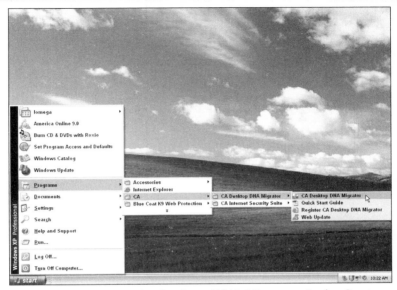

Figure 4-22: Opening CA Desktop DNA Migrator via the Start menu

2. The License Key window should appear. You need an active Internet connection to validate the license key. Ensure you are connected to the Internet, enter the license key, and click Continue.

3. The Welcome screen should appear, as Figure 4-23 shows. Click Next.

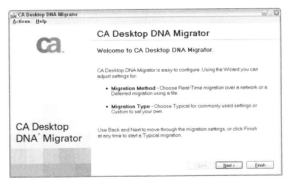

Figure 4-23: Welcome screen

4. Select the Deferred migration method, as shown in Figure 4-24, and click Next.

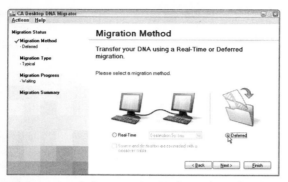

Figure 4-24: Selecting the Deferred method

5. By default, the DNA file is created on the desktop.

If you want to save the DNA file to a different location, enter the alternate path or click Browse to select the location.

Click Next.

6. If you do not want to customize what will be migrated, click Finish to start the migration and continue with Step 7; otherwise follow these steps to customize what will be migrated:

   a. Choose Custom and click Next.

   b. Choose a Migration Type and continue with its steps below:

     You can now specify which items to include in the migration by using the checkboxes. You can also click Edit next to any category to make changes. Then click Finish to start the migration.

7. When the migration is complete, the Migration Summary window, as seen in Figure 4-25, displays the information about the migration.

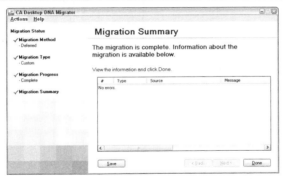

Figure 4-25: The Migration Summary window

Click Done to exit CA Desktop DNA Migrator.

Step 3: Move the DNA

Now you need to move the DNA file you've just created to the new (or destination) PC by using one of the three methods discussed in this section.

Using a CD or DVD

If you have a CD burner, you can burn your DNA file to a writable, or rewritable, CD or DVD. If you have Windows XP, you can use its built-in CD writing features, which the following steps describe:

1. Insert a blank CD or DVD into the drive.

2. Find the DNA file on the source (or old) PC — on the desktop, or you can use My Computer if it's in a different location, as seen in Figure 4-26.

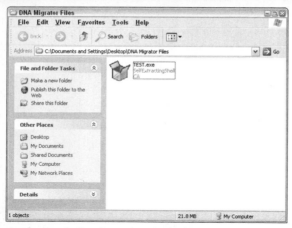

Figure 4-26: Finding the DNA file

3. Open the contents of the CD drive with My Computer, as Figure 4-27 shows.

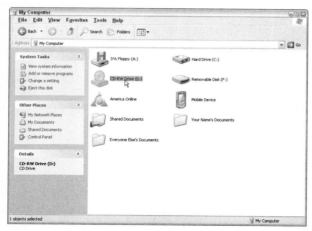

Figure 4-27: Opening the CD drive

4. Drag the DNA file over to the CD drive, as shown in Figure 4-28.

Figure 4-28: Dragging and copying the DNA file

5. Click Write These Files to CD, as shown in Figure 4-29.

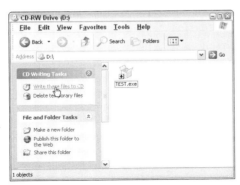

Figure 4-29: Clicking the Write These Files to CD option

The CD or DVD Writing Wizard is displayed.

6. If you would like, you can change the disc's label by editing the CD name field, as in Figure 4-30, and then click Next.

Figure 4-30: Labeling the CD

This starts the writing process. After the writing process is completed, the CD or DVD disc is ejected from the drive.

7. Click Finish, as shown in Figure 4-31, to exit the CD Writing Wizard.

Figure 4-31: Finishing the CD

8. Remove the CD or DVD disc.

9. Insert the disc into the CD or DVD drive of the new PC.

10. Open the contents of CD or DVD drive from My Computer, as Figure 4-32 shows.

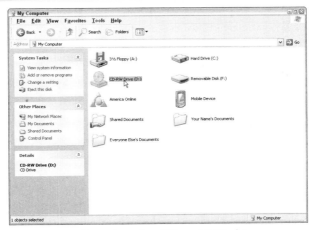

Figure 4-32: Opening the CD or DVD drive

11. Drag the DNA file to the desktop of the new PC, as shown in Figure 4-33, or another desired location.

Figure 4-33: Dragging and copying the DNA file

Using Other Removable Media

You can use other removable media items, such as USB flash or thumb drives. However, check the size of the DNA file to ensure there's enough disk space on the removable media item.

The following describes the process of using a USB flash drive to move the DNA file to the destination (or new) PC with Windows XP:

1. Insert the flash drive into a USB port of the old PC.

2. Find the DNA file on the source (or old) PC such as on the desktop or you can use My Computer if it's in a different location, as seen in Figure 4-34.

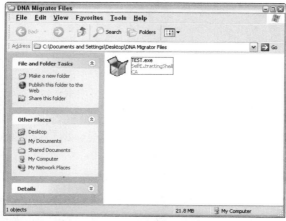

Figure 4-34: Finding the DNA file

3. Open the contents of the flash drive with My Computer, such as Figure 4-35 shows.

Figure 4-35: Opening the flash drive

4. Drag the DNA file over to the flash drive, as shown in Figure 4-36.

Figure 4-36: Dragging and copying the DNA file

5. After the DNA file is done transferring to the flash drive, remove the drive.

6. Insert the flash drive into a USB port of the new PC.

7. Open the contents of the flash drive with My Computer, as Figure 4-37 shows.

Figure 4-37: Opening the flash drive

8. Drag the DNA file to the desktop of the new PC, as shown in Figure 4-38, or another desired location.

Figure 4-38: Dragging and copying the DNA file

Using Your Network

You can use your existing wireless or wired network to move the DNA file to the destination PC, which the following steps describe when using Windows XP:

Note

This assumes your network supports sharing and you have enabled sharing on at least one folder on your destination PC.

1. Make sure both PCs are on the same wireless or wired network and using the same workgroup.

2. Find the DNA file on the source (or old) PC such as on the desktop or you can use My Computer if it's in a different location, as seen in Figure 4-39.

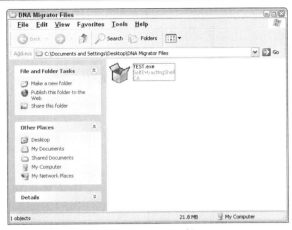

Figure 4-39: Finding the DNA file

3. Double-click My Network Places on your desktop, as Figure 4-40 shows.

Figure 4-40: Opening My Network Places

4. Click View Workgroup Computers, as shown in Figure 4-41.

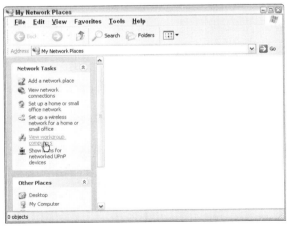

Figure 4-41: Accessing workgroup computers

5. Double-click the computer you would like to transfer the DNA file to, as shown in Figure 4-42.

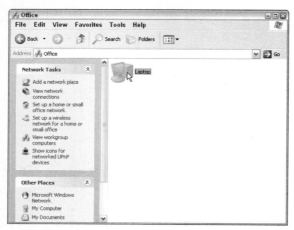

Figure 4-42: Accessing a computer on the network

6. Find and open the folder you would like to transfer the DNA file to, as shown in Figure 4-43.

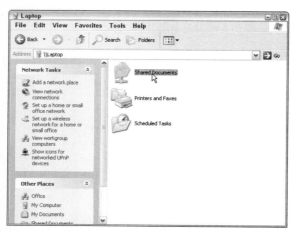

Figure 4-43: Opening a folder on a network computer

7. Drag the DNA file over to the desired folder, as Figure 4-44 shows.

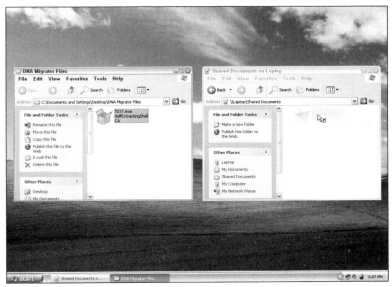

Figure 4-44: Dragging and copying the DNA file

Step 4: Complete the Migration

Follow these steps in order to complete the migration:

1. On your destination (or new) PC, double-click the DNA file, such as shown in Figure 4-45, to automatically load your settings and data from the source (old) PC.

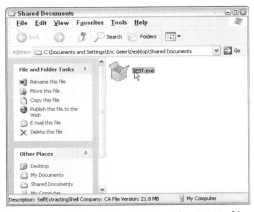

Figure 4-45: Double-clicking the DNA file

2. When the migration is complete, the Migration Summary window, as Figure 4-46 shows, displays the information about your migration.

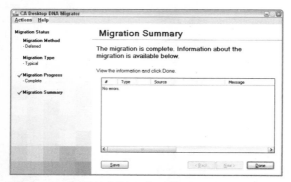

Figure 4-46: The Migration Summary window

Click Done to exit CA Desktop DNA Migrator.

3. You are prompted to restart the PC after the migration is complete.

Click Restart. All migrated settings may not be available until you restart the PC.

The Undo DNA file

During the migration, an Undo DNA file is automatically created on the desktop. This file may be used to undo the settings and data applied during the migration and return the PC back to the pre-migration state. To undo a migration, simply double-click the Undo file on the desktop.

Congratulations, you have successfully completed your migration using CA Desktop DNA Migrator!

5

BACKING UP YOUR FILES

This chapter guides you through the process of backing up your music, photos, settings, and other data using CA Desktop DNA Migrator.

Your Backup Options

There are two main options when it comes to backing up your data:

- **Schedule CA Desktop DNA Migrator**

  Scheduling CA Desktop DNA Migrator to run automatically helps you maintain a current DNA file in case a virus, spyware infection, or any other unexpected problem arises.

  For example, you may accidentally delete important files or they become corrupted; however, if you regularly back up your DNA, you can quickly get the files back.

  Described in a later section, this can be done using Windows Scheduler in Windows XP.

- **Perform a Manual Backup**

  It's also very useful to be able to perform manual backups of your PC. For example, you can capture your PC's DNA and ensure your important files and documents are kept safe before installing software or performing other tasks on your computer that may inadvertently cause havoc.

Scheduling CA Desktop DNA Migrator

The following are steps, which are further discussed in the next sections, you can follow to schedule CA Desktop DNA Migrator to run at specific times:

Step 1: Set Up CA Desktop DNA Migrator as a Scheduled Task

Step 2: Start the Scheduled Backup

Step 3: Archive the DNA File (optional)

Step 1: Set Up CA Desktop DNA Migrator as a Scheduled Task

The following steps show you how to add CA Desktop DNA Migrator to the Windows Scheduler in Windows XP:

1. Open the Control Panel, as seen in Figure 5-1.

Figure 5-1: Opening the Control Panel

If the Start menu is in classic look, the Control Panel is under Settings on the menu.

2. Open the Performance and Maintenance category, as Figure 5-2 shows, if the Control Panel is in category view.

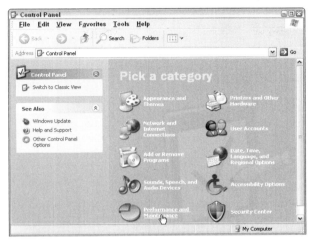

Figure 5-2: Accessing the Performance and Maintenance category

3. Open Scheduled Tasks, as shown in Figure 5-3 when using category view.

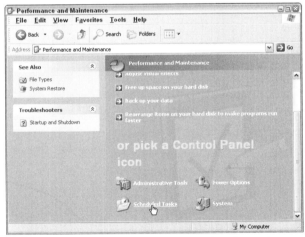

Figure 5-3: Opening the Scheduled Tasks utility

4. Double-click Add Scheduled Task, as Figure 5-4 shows.

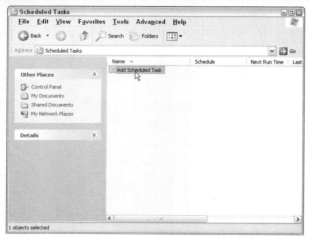

Figure 5-4: Adding a scheduled task

5. After the Scheduled Task Wizard appears, such as Figure 5-5 shows, click Next.

Figure 5-5: Scheduled Task Wizard

6. Scroll through the list of applications, select CA Desktop DNA Migrator, and click Next, such as shown in Figure 5-6.

Figure 5-6: Selecting CA Desktop DNA Migrator

If you cannot locate the application in the list, click Browse and locate C:\Program Files\CA\CA Desktop DNA Migrator. Click DesktopMigrator.exe and click Open.

7. Type a name for this task, such as the example shown in Figure 5-7.

Figure 5-7: Naming the scheduled task

8. Select how often you want to perform a backup and click Next, as Figure 5-8 shows.

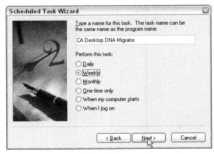

Figure 5-8: Scheduling the task occurrence

9. Select the time and day you want the backup to start, as shown in Figure 5-9.

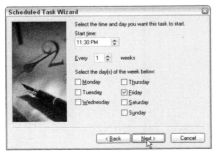

Figure 5-9: Scheduling the task time and day

10. Enter the name and password (if there is one) of the user, such as Figure 5-10 shows, who will be logged on at the time the task runs, and click Next.

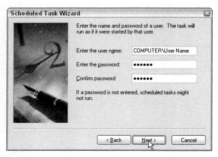

Figure 5-10: Entering user information

11. When you have successfully scheduled the backup, indicated by a window such as shown in Figure 5-11, click Finish.

Figure 5-11: Finished window

Step 2: Start the Scheduled Backup

When the scheduled task runs at the specified time(s) CA Desktop DNA Migrator will open normally. As Figure 5-12 shows, click Finish, and a backup of your PC's DNA will be made.

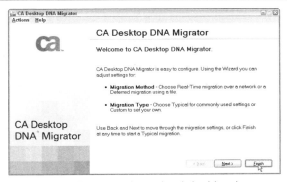

Figure 5-12: Starting the scheduled backup

Do not rename the DNA file so that only the differences made since your last backup (new or edit files) will be saved, thus making the backup more efficient.

You can also manually at any time perform a backup, with Windows Scheduler, outside of your scheduled time:

1. Open the Control Panel, as seen in Figure 5-13.

Figure 5-13: Opening the Control Panel

If the Start menu is in classic look, the Control Panel is under Settings on the menu.

2. Open the Performance and Maintenance category, as Figure 5-14 shows, if the control panel is in category view.

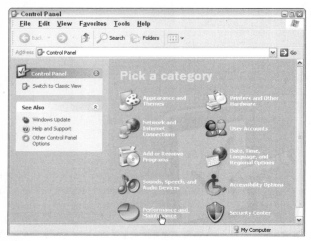

Figure 5-14: Accessing the Performance and Maintenance category

3. Open Scheduled Tasks, as shown in Figure 5-15 when using category view.

Figure 5-15: Opening the Scheduled Tasks utility

4. Right-click the DNA Migrator scheduled task and click Run, such as shown in Figure 5-16.

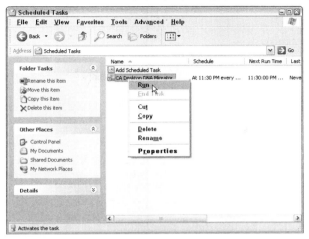

Figure 5-16: Manually running the scheduled task

CA Desktop DNA Migrator will open normally.

5. As Figure 5-17 shows, click Finish and a backup of your PC's DNA will be made.

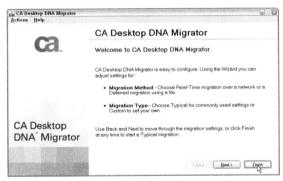

Figure 5-17: Starting the backup

Do not rename the DNA file so that only the differences made since your last backup will be saved, thus making the backup more efficient.

Step 3: Archive the DNA File

It's recommended to save your DNA file to a place other than the source PC, once in a while, after using the Scheduled Backup. Therefore in case you lose all of your data from a system crash or other problem you can simply use a current copy of your PC's DNA, saved on a CD or other safe place, to get the PC and yourself up and running much quicker and hopefully without losing any important files and information.

The following sections describe three methods to safe-keep your DNA files.

Use a CD or DVD

If you have a CD burner, you can burn your DNA file to a writable, or rewritable, CD or DVD. If you have Windows XP, you can use its built-in CD writing features, which the following steps describe:

1. Insert a blank CD or DVD into the drive.

2. Find the DNA file on the source PC, as seen in Figure 5-18.

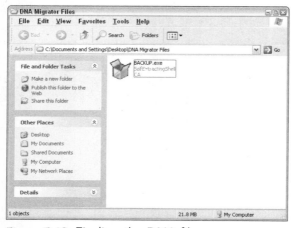

Figure 5-18: Finding the DNA file

By default, the DNA file is created in the DNA Migrator Files folder on the desktop of your computer and named based on the name of your PC.

3. Open the contents of the CD drive with My Computer, such as Figure 5-19 shows.

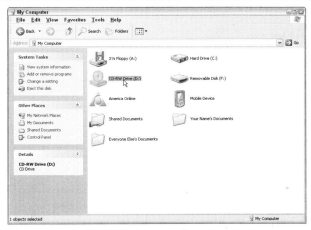

Figure 5-19: Opening the CD drive

4. Drag the DNA file over to the CD drive, as shown in Figure 5-20.

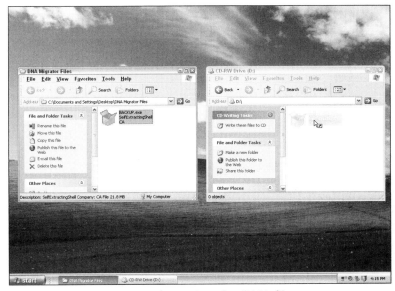

Figure 5-20: Dragging and copying the DNA file

5. Click Write These Files to CD, as shown in Figure 5-21.

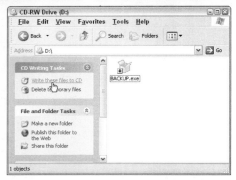

Figure 5-21: Clicking the Write These Files to CD option

The CD or DVD Writing Wizard is displayed.

6. If would like you can change the disc's label by editing the CD name field, such as in Figure 5-22, and click Next.

Figure 5-22: Labeling the CD

This starts the writing process. After the writing process is completed, the CD or DVD disc is ejected from the drive.

7. Click Finish, as shown in Figure 5-23, to exit the CD Writing Wizard.

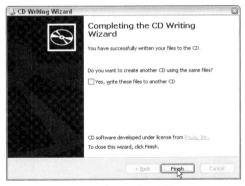

Figure 5-23: Finishing the CD

Use Other Removable Media

You can use other removable media items, such as USB flash or thumb drives. However, check the size of the DNA file to ensure there's enough space on the removable media item.

The following describes the process of saving a DNA file to a USB flash drive when using Windows XP:

1. Insert the flash drive into a USB port of the source PC.

2. Find the DNA file on the source PC, as seen in Figure 5-24.

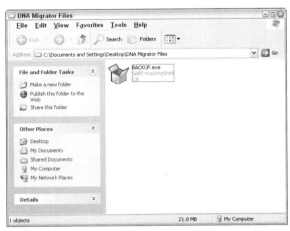

Figure 5-24: Finding the DNA file

By default, the DNA file is created in the DNA Migrator Files folder on the desktop of your computer and named based on the name of your PC.

3. Open the contents of the flash drive with My Computer, such as Figure 5-25 shows.

Figure 5-25: Opening the flash drive

4. Drag the DNA file over to the flash drive, as shown in Figure 5-26.

Figure 5-26: Dragging and copying the DNA file

Use Your Network

You can use an existing wireless or wired network to move the DNA file to another PC, which the following steps describe when using Windows XP:

Note
This assumes your network supports sharing, and you have enabled sharing on at least one folder on your destination PC.

1. Make sure both PCs are on the same wireless or wired network and using the same workgroup.

2. Find the DNA file on the source PC, as seen in Figure 5-27.

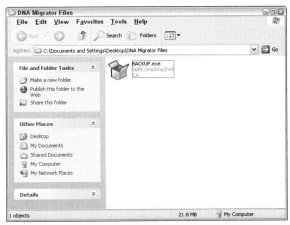

Figure 5-27: Finding the DNA file

By default, the DNA file is created in the DNA Migrator Files folder on the desktop of your computer and named based on the name of your PC.

3. Double-click My Network Places on your desktop, as Figure 5-28 shows.

Figure 5-28: Opening My Network Places

4. Click View Workgroup Computers, as shown in Figure 5-29.

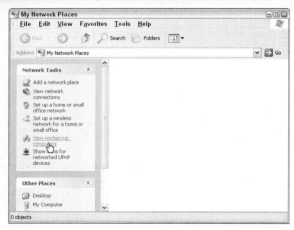

Figure 5-29: Accessing workgroup computers

5. Double-click the computer you would like to transfer the DNA file to, such as shown in Figure 5-30.

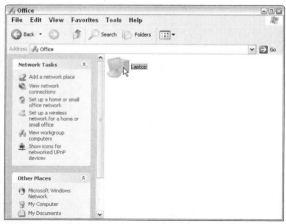

Figure 5-30: Accessing a computer on the network

6. Find and open the folder you would like to transfer the DNA file to, such as seen in Figure 5-31.

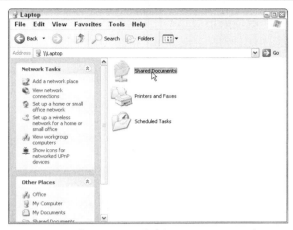

Figure 5-31: Opening a folder on a network computer

7. Drag the DNA file over to the desired folder, as Figure 5-32 shows.

Figure 5-32: Dragging and copying the DNA file

Performing a Manual Backup

The following are the steps to manually create a backup of your DNA and other important files using CA Desktop DNA Migrator, which the next sections discuss in detail:

Step 1: Get Ready

Step 2: Perform the Backup

Step 3: Archive the DNA File (optional)

Step 1: Get Ready

Prepare for the backup by completing these tasks on your PC:

- **Ensure the Software Is Installed**

  If you haven't already, you need to install CA Desktop DNA Migrator. You can refer to Chapter 3 for more information on the installation.

- **Run Anti-virus and Anti-spyware Scans**

  This ensures that you are not backing up any viruses or spyware.

- **Exit All Programs**

  Disable any anti-virus or anti-spyware protection and close all applications on your PC, because they could interfere with the software.

Step 2: Perform the Backup

You can start the backup process by creating your DNA file:

1. Open CA Desktop DNA Migrator, which can be accessed by browsing to the following path on your Start menu:

   Programs (or All Programs) → CA → CA Desktop DNA Migrator

   Then click CA Desktop DNA Migrator, as shown in Figure 5-33.

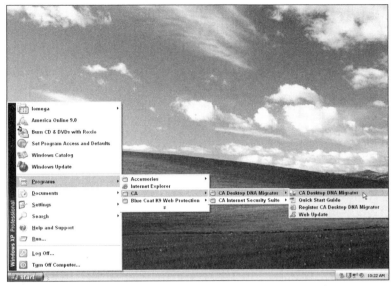

Figure 5-33: Opening CA Desktop DNA Migrator via the Start menu

Note

The first time you run the software, the License Key window should appear and you need an active Internet connection in order to validate the license key.

Ensure you are connected to the Internet and enter the license key, and click Continue.

2. The Welcome screen should appear, as Figure 5-34 shows. Click Next.

Figure 5-34: Welcome screen

3. Select the Deferred method, as shown in Figure 5-35, and click Next.

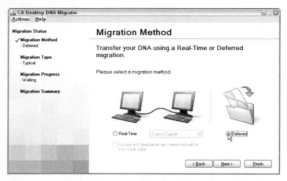

Figure 5-35: Selecting the Deferred method

4. By default, the DNA file is created on the desktop.

If you want to save the DNA file to a different location, enter the alternate path or click Browse to select the location.

Click Next.

5. If you do not want to customize what will be backed up, click Finish to start the backup and continue with Step 6; otherwise, follow these steps to customize what will be backed up:

    a. Choose Custom and click Next.

    b. Choose a Migration Type and continue with its steps below:

        You can now specify which items to include in the migration by using the checkboxes. You can also click Edit next to any category to make changes. Then click Finish to start the migration.

6. When the backup is complete, the Migration Summary window, as seen in Figure 5-36, displays the information about the backup.

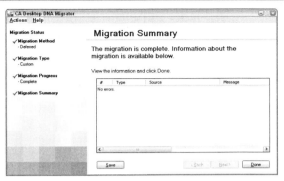

Figure 5-36: The Migration Summary window

Click Done to exit CA Desktop DNA Migrator.

Step 3: Archive the DNA File

It's recommended to save your DNA file to a place other than the source PC in case you lose all the data from a system crash or other problem. Therefore, you can simply use a current copy of your PC's DNA, saved on a CD or other safe place, to get the PC and yourself up and running much quicker and hopefully without losing any important files and information.

The following sections describe three methods to safe-keep your DNA files.

Use a CD or DVD

If you have a CD burner, you can burn your DNA file to a writable, or rewritable, CD or DVD. If you have Windows XP, you can use its built-in CD writing features, which the following steps describe:

1. Insert a blank CD or DVD into the drive.

2. Find the DNA file on the source (or old) PC such as on the desktop or you can use My Computer if it's in different location, as seen in Figure 5-37.

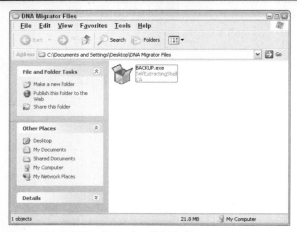

Figure 5-37: Finding the DNA file

3. Open the contents of the CD drive with My Computer, such as Figure 5-38 shows.

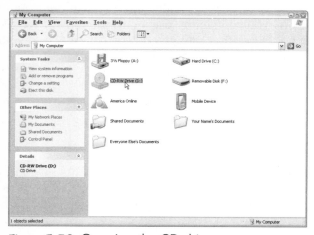

Figure 5-38: Opening the CD drive

4. Drag the DNA file over to the CD drive, as shown in Figure 5-39.

Figure 5-39: Dragging and copying the DNA file

5. Click Write These Files to CD, as shown in Figure 5-40.

Figure 5-40: Clicking the Write These Files to CD option

The CD or DVD Writing Wizard is displayed.

6. If would like you can change the disc's label by editing the CD name field, such as in Figure 5-41, and click Next.

Figure 5-41: Labeling the CD

This starts the writing process. After the writing process is completed, the CD or DVD disc is ejected from the drive.

7. Click Finish, as shown in Figure 5-42, to exit the CD Writing Wizard.

Figure 5-42: Finishing the CD

Use Other Removable Media

You can use other removable media items, such as USB flash or thumb drives. However, check the size of the DNA file to ensure there's enough disk space on the removable media item.

The following describes the process of saving a DNA file to a USB flash drive when using Windows XP:

1. Insert the flash drive into a USB port of the old PC.

2. Find the DNA file on the source (or old) PC such as on the desktop or you can use My Computer if it's in different location, as seen in Figure 5-43.

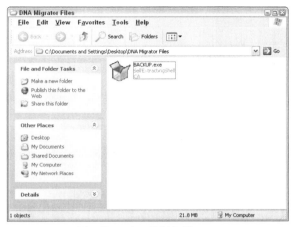

Figure 5-43: Finding the DNA file

3. Open the contents of the flash drive with My Computer, such as Figure 5-44 shows.

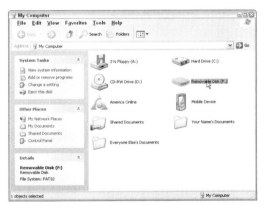

Figure 5-44: Opening the flash drive

4. Drag the DNA file over to the flash drive, as shown in Figure 5-45.

Figure 5-45: Dragging and copying the DNA file

Use Your Network

You can use an existing wireless or wired network to move the DNA file to another PC, which the following steps describe when using Windows XP:

Note

This assumes your network supports sharing, and you have enabled sharing on at least one folder on your destination PC.

1. Make sure both PCs are on the same the wireless or wired network and using the same workgroup.

2. Find the DNA file on the source PC such as on the desktop or you can use My Computer if it's in different location, as seen in Figure 5-46.

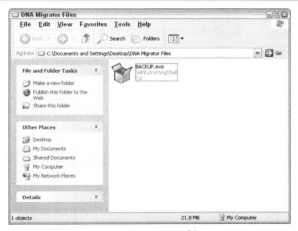

Figure 5-46: Finding the DNA file

3. Double-click My Network Places on your desktop, as Figure 5-47 shows.

Figure 5-47: Opening My Network Places

4. Click View Workgroup Computers, as shown in Figure 5-48.

Figure 5-48: Accessing workgroup computers

5. Double-click the computer you would like to transfer the DNA file to, such as shown in Figure 5-49.

Figure 5-49: Accessing a computer on the network

6. Find and open the folder you would like to transfer the DNA file to, such as seen in Figure 5-50.

Figure 5-50: Opening a folder on a network computer

7. Drag the DNA file over to the desired folder, such as Figure 5-51 shows.

Figure 5-51: Dragging and copying the DNA file

6

RESTORING YOUR PC WITH YOUR DNA BACKUP

If your PC crashes or you run into other unexpected issues, such as finding out that a week ago you deleted a important file from your PC, and you have been backing up your PC with CA Desktop DNA Migrator you're in luck — this chapter explains how you can easily restore your saved files, settings, and other important information!

Find the DNA File

First you need to find the DNA file that contains the files and settings you would like to restore. CA Desktop DNA Migrator by default creates the DNA in a folder named DNA Migrator Files on the desktop of your computer, as Figure 6-1 shows.

Figure 6-1: The DNA Migrator Files folder

The default name of the DNA file is based on the name of your PC, as shown in Figure 6-2.

Figure 6-2: Example of a DNA file

If the DNA file you would like to use isn't located in the default location, you can find the file by browsing your PC using My Computer or Windows Explorer.

Restore Your PC's DNA

After you find the DNA file continue with these steps:

1. Double-click the DNA file, as shown in Figure 6-3, to restore your settings and data.

Figure 6-3: Double-clicking the DNA file

CA Desktop DNA Migrator should start and begin the process, as shown in Figure 6-4.

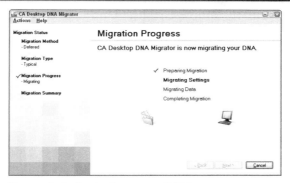

Figure 6-4: Restoring your DNA

2. When the backup is complete, the Migration Summary window, as Figure 6-5 shows, displays information about your backup.

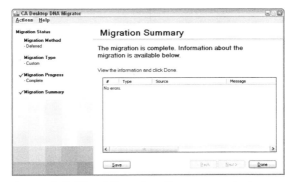

Figure 6-5: The Migration Summary window

Click Done to exit CA Desktop DNA Migrator.

3. You are prompted to restart the PC after the migration is complete.

Click Restart. All migrated settings may not be available until you restart the PC.

Undo Restored DNA

During a restore, an Undo DNA file is automatically created on the desktop. This file may be used to undo the settings and data applied during the restore and return the PC back to the pre-restore state.

To undo the restore, simply double-click the Undo file on the desktop, as shown in Figure 6-6.

Figure 6-6: Undoing the backup

7

UPDATING YOUR SOFTWARE

To ensure you get the most out of CA Desktop DNA Migrator, you should keep the software up to date with any fixes or new features, which may include the migration and backup support of more system and application settings. Therefore, you should check for updates once in a while as described in this chapter.

Using the Start Menu

You can quickly check for updates by using the Start menu shortcut:

1. Open the Web Update utility, which can be accessed by browsing to the following path on your Start menu:

   Programs (or All Programs) → CA → CA Desktop DNA Migrator

2. Then click Web Update, as shown in Figure 7-1.

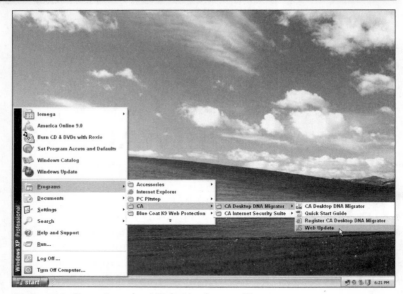

Figure 7-1: Opening the Web Update utility

The Web Update utility should load.

Note

If you are using firewall protection, you may receive an alert informing you that the Web Update application is trying to access the Internet, as Figure 7-2 shows when using CA Personal Firewall.

If you receive an alert similar to this or if the utility isn't able to access the Internet, make sure you authorize the application to go through the firewall.

If the CA Desktop DNA Migrator software is currently open, you'll receive a status message such as shown in Figure 7-2, and you need to close the software in order to continue.

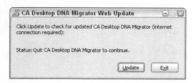

Figure 7-2: Status message to close CA Desktop DNA Migrator

3. Once the status says Ready to Update, as shown in Figure 7-3, you can click Update to begin.

Figure 7-3: Ready to Update status message

The WebUpdate Automatic Updater window, such as shown in Figure 7-4, should appear and begin to check for updates and install any new ones.

Figure 7-4: WebUpdate Automatic Updater window

If there aren't any new updates available, you'll receive a pop-up message such as shown in Figure 7-5.

Figure 7-5: No Updates Needed pop-up message

Using the Software

You can also access the update utility within the CA Desktop DNA Migrator software:

1. Open CA Desktop DNA Migrator, which can be accessed by browsing to the following path on your Start menu:

Programs (or All Programs) → CA → CA Desktop DNA Migrator

Then click CA Desktop DNA Migrator, as shown in Figure 7-6.

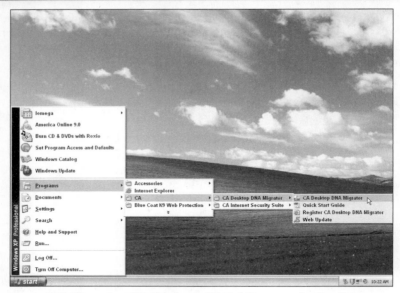

Figure 7-6: Opening CA Desktop DNA Migrator via the Start menu

2. Under the Actions toolbar menu click Web Update, as Figure 7-7 shows.

Figure 7-7: Accessing the Web Update utility

The Web Update utility should load.

Note

If you are using firewall protection, you may receive an alert informing you that the Web Update application is trying to access the Internet, as Figure 7-8 shows when using CA Personal Firewall.

If you receive an alert similar to this or if the utility isn't able to access the Internet, make sure you authorize the application to go through the firewall.

If the CA Desktop DNA Migrator software is currently open, you'll receive a status message as shown in Figure 7-8 and you need to close the software in order to continue.

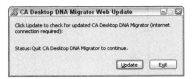

Figure 7-8: Status message to close CA Desktop DNA Migrator

3. Once the status says Ready to Update, as shown in Figure 7-9, you can click Update to begin.

Figure 7-9: Ready to Update status message

The WebUpdate Automatic Updater window, as shown in Figure 7-10, should appear and begin to check for updates and install any new ones.

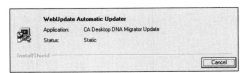

Figure 7-10: WebUpdate Automatic Updater window

If there aren't any new updates available, you'll receive a pop-up message such as shown in Figure 7-11.

Figure 7-11: No Updates Needed pop-up message

8

TROUBLESHOOTING

This chapter discusses common problems and fixes you may experience when using CA Desktop DNA Migrator and also lets you know where you can get more help.

Cannot Find a Source System

Problem:

When performing a Real-Time migration, the destination PC cannot find a Source System or the Source System is not listed; however, the Source System is running.

Fixes:

- **Check Network or Cable Connections**

  Make sure that you are connected to the same wired or wireless network or directly to the Source System with a crossover cable. You can usually check the status of your network connections by hovering over the network connection system tray icon, when using Windows XP, as shown in Figure 8-1.

  Figure 8-1: Viewing network connection status via the system tray icon

- **When using a wireless network**

  To ensure both PCs are on the same wireless network, you should check each computer to see what network name (or SSID) they're connected to, as shown in Figure 8-1.

- **When using a wired network**

  To ensure both PCs are on the same wired (or Ethernet) network, you should check the Local Area Network connection status, as shown in Figure 8-1, on each computer and verify the physical connection of the two PCs via their Ethernet cards.

- **When using a crossover cable**

  To ensure a proper connection when using a crossover cable, you should check the Local Area Network connection status on each computer, as shown in Figure 8-1.

- **Check Subnet Mask**

  If you are connected, either via a wireless or wired network or direct connection via a crossover cable, make sure that both systems are on the same subnet.

  You can do this by accessing the status window for the network connection by double-clicking the system tray icon, as shown earlier in Figure 8-1, and viewing the IP address on the Support tab, as shown in Figure 8-2.

Figure 8-2: Network Connection Status window Support tab

If both IP address have the same numbers except the last set, for example, 192.168.1.100 and 192.168.1.101, then the systems are on the same subnet.

- **Check Firewall**

  If you have verified the first two items, an active firewall may be interfering with the CA Desktop DNA Migrator software. Make sure you have disabled all firewall protection.

Wrong Source System

Problem:

The destination did not connect to the correct Source System.

Fix:

When clicking Finish on the Welcome window or the Migration Method window of the Destination System, CA Desktop DNA Migrator will connect to the first Source System that it can find. To connect to a different source use the Source Selection page.

Desktop Picture Not Migrated

Problem:

The desktop picture did not get migrated or restored.

Fix:

This is most likely a problem with the active desktop settings.

You can change the desktop picture back and change any of the display properties by following these steps, when using Windows XP:

1. Right-click the desktop and click Properties, as shown in Figure 8-3.

Figure 8-3: Accessing display properties

2. Click the Desktop tab, as Figure 8-4 shows.

Figure 8-4: Windows desktop properties

3. You can scroll through the background images or use the Browse button to select a different image.

4. When you're done, click OK.

Unexpected Application Settings Result

Problem:

Unexpected application settings result after the migration is complete.

Fix:

Only the settings for applications that are installed on the Source System are included in the migration. If you performed a Custom migration, verify that you selected the required settings.

Customer Support Information

For any other problems or specific questions, you can contact CA's Customer Support by visiting its website:

`http://www.ca.com/home/support/`

PART III
BONUS MATERIAL

In This Part

The main use of CA Desktop DNA Migrator is to transfer your PC's files and DNA to a new computer, which was covered in Part 2 of this book. In addition, we felt that it would very beneficial for you to have some additional tips that will make the experience with your new PC a good one. Therefore, included in this part of the book are bonus chapters that cover many applications and topics that you may be concerned or involved with after getting a new PC.

This part of the book ensures that you understand some of the latest technologies, such as wireless (or Wi-Fi) networking, and that you are briefed on the digital dangers of using the Internet, because you'll likely spend much more time online if you have recently upgraded to a high-speed Internet connection. In addition, this part of the book discusses many popular recent software titles that may have come pre-installed on your new PC or that you may discover and purchase at your local computing store.

This additional bonus material is concisely written and covers the main elements that you need to know. This saves you lots of money by avoiding the need to purchase separate books on these topics. We just want to be sure that you get the best out of your new PC!

9

AFTER MIGRATING
TO A NEW PC

E ven though you may be done with the migration
of your files and DNA to your new computer,
there are a few things you should address, such
as how to dispose of your old PC and what you can do
to keep your new PC running smoothly.

What to Do with Your Old Computer

After you've migrated to a new computer, you need to
decide what to do with the old clunker. The following
sections give you some ideas so it's not just another
addition to your heap of stuff in the basement.

Give It to the Kids

If you have children of your own or others in your
family, think about giving the old PC to them. This
will provide them with a computer of their own that
they can tinker with, and you won't have to be on
edge thinking about them using the brand-new PC
you just spent hundreds or thousands of dollars on
and that's loaded with all your personal files.

You could load their games on the old computer,
which shouldn't be a problem; however, you need to
keep in mind the system requirements of the particular games before you get them at the store. Some of
the newer games will have operating system and memory requirements that exceed those of the old PC. In
this case, you might consider upgrading your old PC.

You could also set up the PC with an Internet connection so the child has quick access to the Internet for homework and other online activities. If you aren't familiar yet with wireless home networking, check it out. You can set up a network so all the computers in your home share a high-speed Internet connection, which is relativity quick and inexpensive.

Upgrade It

You can upgrade your old computer if you do decide to keep it as an additional PC or you want to bring it up to speed before giving it to someone else. If you aren't comfortable doing computer upgrades, you can always take the PC to a local computer repair store, and they'll fix you up.

Diagnosing Computer Problems

If you are willing to do it yourself, you need to figure out what to upgrade. Here are some common PC problems and the hardware or software upgrades that might fix them:

- **Problem:** The computer takes an unusually long time to start up, to shut down, or to open programs and folders. Also, the computer feels sluggish.

  Solution: Upgrade to a faster processor (CPU), or add more system memory (RAM).

- **Problem:** The computer frequently freezes or crashes, often resulting in error messages or blue screens displaying strange text.

  Solution: Update or reinstall Windows, or add more system memory (RAM).

- **Problem:** Messages warn that the computer is running low on disk space or doesn't have enough room to install a program.

  Solution: Upgrade to a larger hard drive, or add a second hard drive.

Commonly Upgraded Components

Here are some suggestions regarding computer components that owners typically replace or buy when upgrading:

- **Newer Windows**

  If you are using an outdated version of Windows such as 95, 98, or ME, consider upgrading to the most recent version. Windows XP or newer operating systems make it much easier to use peripherals such as digital cameras and printers, to connect to wireless networks, and so much more.

  But above all else, a newer Windows is usually more stable and safe than its predecessors, which means you won't have to endure the frequent "blue screens of death" that plague Windows 95 and 98.

- **RAM (Memory)**

  An inexpensive way to add some zip to your computer is to install more system memory (RAM). Along with the extra speed, you will be able to use more programs at the same time, such as checking email while surfing the Internet while listening to digital music files.

- **Hard Drive**

  If your computer is several years old, you probably have a small hard drive that is quickly running out of storage space. Replacing your current hard drive or adding an additional one will give you ample room to store your growing collection of documents, digital photos, digital music, videos, and software.

  If you aren't a do-it-yourselfer, the easiest way to add extra storage to your crowded computer is to buy an external hard drive. Basically this device is a standard hard drive enclosed in a rugged plastic or metal case that protects it from being damaged. The best thing is that it connects to your computer through USB or FireWire ports — which means you don't have to open your computer's case and tinker with its internal components.

- **USB Card**

  USB is the type of connection used by almost all computer peripherals including printers, digital cameras, and scanners. If you have an older computer that lacks USB ports — or if you need extra ports — you can install a USB card.

- **FireWire Card**

  FireWire is another type of high-speed connection used by many computer peripherals such as external hard drives and video cameras. However, FireWire is not used with as many peripherals as USB. Similar to USB, FireWire capabilities can be added to a computer by installing a special card.

- **CD or DVD Drive**

  Have you ever wanted to watch a DVD movie on your computer or make your own custom music CDs? With a modern CD or DVD drive, both activities are possible — and much more. Here are the different types of CD or DVD drives currently available:

  - **Read-Only:** These drives can only read information on prerecorded discs. Examples include CD-ROM and DVD-ROM.

  - **Recordable or rewritable:** These drives can read data on prerecorded discs and write (or "burn") data onto blank discs. Examples include CD-R, CD-RW, DVD-R, DVD-RW, DVD+R, and DVD+RW. Most of these drives are restricted to using one type of disc. That means "minus R" (-R) drives cannot use "plus R" (+R) discs, and vice versa.

  - **Combo drives:** These drives can read and burn data on any type of disc. They are an ideal choice for people who don't want to worry about what type of discs to buy.

- **Network Card**

  To connect to a high-speed Internet service such as DSL or cable, your computer typically must have a wired network card (also called an Ethernet card) or a wireless network card (also called a Wi-Fi card).

- **Video Card**

  A video card is the important piece of hardware that sends images from your computer to your monitor. If the bulk of your computer activities involve the use of programs such as Microsoft Word, Outlook, and Internet Explorer, you don't need a powerful video card. However, if you want to play the newest PC video games that have cutting-edge graphics, you will need to upgrade to a fast video card.

- **Sound Card**

  If you enjoy playing video games or watching DVD movies on your computer, you should consider upgrading your sound card to one that has enhanced features such as Dolby Digital 5.1 or 7.1 surround sound.

Donate It

You could also donate your old PC to a charity, church, school, or other non-profit organization and possibility claim the donation on your taxes. For individuals, this should work as long as you itemize your deductions. Then you can write off the Fair Market Value (FMV) of the computer, which you can estimate from the following websites:

- `http://www.usedprice.com/`
- `http://servlets.edeal.com/servlets/PcEval`

Recycle It

Most computer manufacturers take old PCs off your hands for free or even give you money back for trading in when you purchase a new computer. Following is a list of where to find information on the recycling programs for some of the popular computer manufacturers:

- Dell — `www.dell.com/us/en/dhs/topics/segtopic_dell_recycling.htm`
- Gateway — `gateway.eztradein.com/gateway/`
- HP — `hp.com/hpinfo/globalcitizenship/environment/recycle/index.html`
- IBM — `www.ibm.com/financing/us/recovery/small/`

Sell It

You may even be able to get a few bucks from an old PC. You can check with the local computer and second-time around stores in your area. You could also check into listing the item in the classified ads or trading post, if you feel it's worthwhile.

You may also consider using a reputable website where it's possible to sell used computers. There you can see what others are listing their computers for and what they are actually getting for them. Don't forget about shipping costs, which may be relatively high due to the size and weight of the box.

Throw It Away

Just getting rid of an old PC isn't as simple as kicking it to the curb on trash day. Because PCs are not biodegradable, throwing them in the trash may not be very good for Mother Earth. Some states have even outlawed the disposal of computer waste in landfills.

However, there are some places you can dump your old computer and electronic gear. The Electronic Equipment Recyclers organization provides a directory of these places online at www.nsc.org/ehc/epr2/recycler.htm.

Erasing Data from a PC

When deleting files on your computer, even from the Recycle Bin, they're not actually gone forever. There are special software tools that can recover deleted files and documents. Although this is very useful if used in the right situation, criminals can also retrieve this discarded information.

To protect your personal information, such as passwords, credit card numbers, and other previously deleted data, you need to permanently wipe out this data before giving your PC away to someone else.

Keeping Your New PC Healthy

Junk files and some other not-so-obvious things, such as disk errors and clutter, can cause poor PC performance. To keep your new PC up and running smoothly you should perform regular maintenance and take preventative measures, such as the following sections discuss.

Note
For more information on how to perform the maintenance recommended in this section you can refer to another book in this series, *Simple Computer Tune-up: Speed Up Your PC.*

Keep Windows Up to Date

Microsoft releases periodic updates for Windows to ensure your PC is protected from the latest known security holes and programming bugs or errors. Many of these updates will help increase your PC's performance. In addition, an out-of-date Windows may comprise the security and performance of your PC.

Remove Unused Files and Programs

Unused programs and files are one of the biggest contributors to wasted disk space and can cause a reduction in your PC's perform-ance. As a general rule of thumb, the less disk space you use of your hard drive, the better overall PC performance you'll experience. Therefore, it's best to remove software programs that aren't used and files that you don't need anymore.

Delete Temporary Files

Computers naturally create many different temporary files, which are typically stored for your advantage. However, these temporary files on your computer can stack up, which can contribute to poor PC performance. Therefore, periodically delete these temporary files to keep your new PC healthy.

The following are the main temporary files:

- **Internet Cache**

  Web browsers (for example, Internet Explorer) typically create temporary files, often referred to as Internet Cache, during web browsing. These temporary files usually aren't needed after you are finished surfing the web, and they can take up large amounts of space on your hard drive.

- **Recycle Bin**

  Remember, files are not actually removed from the hard drive when you delete them the first time. For instance, deleting files for the first time actually sends them to the Recycle Bin. Then from there you can either remove them from your computer or in case you figured out that they should not have been deleted, you can restore them.

- **Windows Temporary Files**

  The Windows operating system and other applications cre-ate temporary files for various reasons, such as during soft-ware installations. These temporary files, however, are typically not needed after the application exits or when Windows is shut down.

Keep Your Personal Files Organized

Organizing personal files and documents that are scattered through-out your PC and deleting old or unused files will help free up disk space. In addition, this helps keep your PC healthy.

- **Create separate personal folders**

  Start with creating folders for each user of your PC. For example, if it's a family PC you may want to create a separate folder for each member in a convenient place such as the desktop or My Documents.

  This way everyone has a place to save and create their documents, which helps keep the files on your computer organized.

- **Create sub-folders**

  Then you can create sub-folders, for each of your topics or interests, for each computer user.

- **Periodically clean up your files**

  Once in a while you should go through your folders and delete any files you don't need anymore. Especially look for and remove large files.

Maintain Your Hard Drive

Data in hard drives can become corrupt and contain errors, such as from the following situations:

- Improper shutdown from power outage
- Power surges
- PC suddenly resets (bad power connection or supply)
- PC crashes or locks up, so that shutdown is impossible

When there are errors in a hard drive, it can't work at its optimum performance. Typically, hard drive errors won't be noticeable to the PC user, which makes the situation even worse. Therefore, make sure you periodically perform hard drive checks.

Fragmentation of your hard drive is also a concern. Fragmentation is the condition in which files are divided into pieces scattered around a hard drive and can have a significant impact on PC performance. This is because it takes more time to access files on a hard drive if they are fragmented.

The following are causes of fragmentation:

- Installing software
- Uninstalling software
- Moving files
- Deleting files

Even though fragmentation is common and occurs naturally, there are ways to help the problem, which are discussed in a later chapter.

Watch Those Start-up Programs

Many software programs may add themselves (with or without your knowledge) to your Startup folder, which may cause a longer boot time when entering Windows.

Additionally, these programs running in the background will steal computing power from other applications you are using and will overall bog down your PC.

10

CONNECTING TO THE INTERNET

In the blink of an eye, the Internet — also referred to as the "web" — has gone from novelty to necessity, ingraining itself in our culture to such an extent that people don't just use it — they depend on it. For some, life without the web is inconceivable. After using CA's Desktop DNA Migrator to transfer files to a new PC, you'll need to interface your new computer to the Internet. This chapter shows you how to deal with some of the problems that you might encounter.

- Using email to stay in contact with family, friends, and business associates

- Saving money by shopping at e-merchants (Internet stores)

- Managing bank accounts

- Paying bills directly from a checking account

- Doing research for school and work-related projects

- Reading the latest news headlines from the Associated Press or CNN

- Checking sports scores and movie show times

- Downloading "try-it-before-you-buy-it" versions of software

- Purchasing legal digital copies of music CDs and individual songs

- Viewing streaming videos of concerts, sporting events, and breaking news

Types of Internet Service

If you haven't yet taken a dip in the vast digital ocean known as the Internet, what are you waiting for? The first step you must take is to decide what type of Internet service fits your needs and your budget. The three types of Internet used in most homes and small businesses are dial-up, DSL (which stands for digital subscriber line), and cable.

Note
DSL and cable Internet services are usually referred to as "broadband."

Dial-up Internet Service

- Uses regular telephone lines

- Requires a dial-up modem (which most computers have)

- Is available in any home or office that has a working telephone line

- Has a very slow connection speed (up to 56K)

- Is inexpensive, costing between $10 and $22 per month (depending on whether your plan has a limited number of hours per month or has unlimited usage)

DSL Internet Service

- Uses regular telephone lines

- Requires a USB or Ethernet port on your PC

- Is available in many larger communities but is not always offered in smaller ones

- Has a medium connection speed (between 300K and 800K, depending on how far away your home or office is from a DSL transmitter)

- Is reasonably priced, costing between $15 and $30 per month

Cable Internet Service

- Uses cable lines to transmit signals (the same lines that provide cable TV)

- Requires a USB or Ethernet port on your PC

- Is not available in every community (but is usually offered in more areas than DSL)

- Has a fast connection speed (up to 1,500K)
- Is more expensive, costing between $45 and $50 per month

Sign Up for Internet Service

After you have decided what type of Internet access you prefer, you need to sign up for an account with an Internet service provider (ISP). For dial-up, this usually can be done without professional help. For DSL and cable, it either requires professional installation or a do-it-yourself kit offered by the Internet provider.

Dial-up Internet Access

Numerous local and national companies offer dial-up Internet services. When selecting a dial-up provider, consider these features:

- **Amount of access numbers:** Make sure the provider offers several local access numbers near your home or office (because if you don't dial a local number, you could be charged for making expensive long-distance calls every time you connect to the Internet). Also, choose a provider that offers more than one local access number. That way, if one number is busy, you can always call another.

- **Price:** Compare the monthly fees charged by each provider for unlimited Internet access.

- **Number of email accounts:** Most dial-up providers allow you to have several email accounts — enough for each person in your household or small business.

- **Website space:** Many dial-up providers give you a specific amount of space to create your own website that can be accessed by anyone who uses the Internet. This is particularly useful if you run a small or home-based business.

When you have chosen a dial-up provider, follow these steps to set up an account:

1. If you have decided to go with a national dial-up company, you will need to obtain a CD containing its installation software. Usually these CDs can be picked up free of charge at most computer or electronics stores. If no stores in your area carry them, ask your neighbors if they have any. If you still have no luck, use a computer at your office

or at a neighbor's house to visit the dial-up provider's website and sign up for service as well as download the installation software.

2. If you have decided to go with a local dial-up company, you must call it to inquire about how to sign up. Usually the company sends a technician to perform the setup or mails you an installation CD.

3. Connect your modem to a telephone jack by plugging one end of a telephone cord into your modem and then plugging the other end into a telephone jack on the wall of your home or office.

4. Install the dial-up software and follow the on-screen instructions.

DSL Internet Service

Because DSL Internet services use a traditional telephone line, they are usually offered by your local phone company. Here is a general overview of the steps involved in setting up DSL:

1. Scan your local telephone directory to determine which phone companies in your area offer DSL. If you have more than one choice, compare their prices, features, and customer service before making a decision.

2. After you have picked a provider, sign up for a DSL account. Most DSL providers can install the necessary equipment — for a fee. To save money, ask for a self-installation kit. Typically, this kit contains a DSL modem, Ethernet cables, phone-line filters, an installation CD, and detailed instructions.

Cable Internet Service

As its name indicates, cable Internet services are offered by a local cable company (the same one that provides your local cable TV channels). Many communities have only a single cable provider, but a lucky few have more than one (which helps to drive down the cost of the cable services). Here is a general overview of the steps involved in setting up cable Internet:

1. Scan your local telephone directory to determine which companies in your area offer cable Internet. If you have more than one choice, compare their prices, features, and customer service before making a decision.

2. After you have picked a provider, sign up for an Internet account. Most cable providers can install the necessary equipment—for a fee. To save money, ask for a self-installation kit. Typically, this kit contains a cable modem, Ethernet cables, an installation CD, and detailed instructions.

Restore a Dial-up Connection

If your modem suddenly cannot access your dial-up Internet service, try these fixes:

- **Check for a dial tone:** Use a standard telephone to call the local access number that your modem is trying to dial. Within a few seconds you should hear a digital tone. If you don't hear it, either you called the wrong number or your Internet provider's equipment is not working properly. If you hear a busy signal, try using your modem to dial an alternate local access number.

- **Check your modem's status:** If you are certain that the local access number is working properly, you should determine whether your modem has malfunctioned. See the section that follows for details.

For Windows XP and Windows 2000

1. Click the Start button in the lower-left corner of Windows.

2. Click the Control Panel. (If you don't see this option, your start menu is in classic mode. In that case, click Settings, and then select the Control Panel.)

3. If the Control Panel is in category view, click the Performance and Maintenance category, and then click the System icon. If the Control Panel is in classic view, simply double-click the System icon.

4. A window opens. Click the Hardware tab.

5. Click the Device Manager button.

6. The Device Manager window opens. Click the plus sign (+) next to the Modems category.

7. Double-click the name of your modem.

8. Another window opens. On the General tab, look for the Device status heading. There you should see a message indicating whether or not your modem is working properly.

9. If the message says your modem is not working properly or has an error, try uninstalling the software that came with your modem. Next, reinstall that same software, and then try using the modem again.

10. If the message says your modem is operating correctly, check to see if your connection problems have occurred because the telephone cord is loose or unplugged from either the modem or the phone jack. Also, check for cuts, splits, or large dents on the phone cord. If it is damaged, replace it, and then try your Internet connection again.

11. If your connection problems continue, replace your modem.

For Windows 98 and Windows ME

1. Right-click the My Computer icon on your desktop.

2. Select Properties.

3. Click the Device Manager tab.

4. The Device Manager window opens. Click the plus sign (+) next to the Modem category.

5. Double-click the name of your modem.

6. Another window opens. On the General tab, look for the Device status heading. There you should see a message indicating whether or not your modem is working properly.

7. If the message says your modem is not working properly or has an error, try uninstalling the software that came with your modem. Next, reinstall that same software, and then try using the modem again.

8. If the message says your modem is operating correctly, check to see if your connection problems have occurred because the telephone cord is loose or unplugged from either the modem or the phone jack. Also, check for cuts, splits, or large dents on the phone cord. If it is damaged, replace it, and then try your Internet connection again.

9. If your connection problems continue, replace your modem.

Note

For dial-up Internet connections, use telephone cords shorter than 15 feet. Anything longer will degrade the signal quality and produce a slower Internet connection.

Troubleshoot a Slow Dial-up Connection

If your dial-up Internet feels unusually slow, try one of these remedies:

1. Try dialing an alternate access number. It is possible that your current access number has slowed because a large number of people are using it simultaneously.

2. Inspect your phone cord for cuts, splits, or large dents. If the cord is damaged, replace it, and then try your Internet connection again.

3. If your current phone cord is quite long, replace it with one that is as short as possible (because shorter phone cords often provide faster dial-up connections).

4. If you hear annoying static while making phone calls, there is a good chance the static is also interfering with the signals your dial-up modem sends and receives. Ask your phone company to repair the line and eliminate the static.

Note

Be wary of software that claims to boost the speed of your Internet connection, unless, like PC Pitstop Optimizer, it's from a proven software company. Known as a *Web accelerator*, *Internet accelerator*, or *Internet optimizer*, this type of program can damage Windows and prevent you from connecting to the Web. If you currently use a slow, dial-up Internet connection and need more speed, try PC Pitstop Optimize. The only other solution is to sign up for a broadband service such as cable or DSL that is offered by your local cable and phone companies.

Access the Internet from a Wired Network

If your PC has a network card (also called an Ethernet card), you can use it to connect to a wired computer network that has been set up in your home or office or in a place like a hotel room.

Note

If you are connecting to a public network (such as those found in hotel rooms, coffee shops, and so on), you don't have to dial in to the Internet provider you use back home.

1. Obtain an Ethernet cable (often called a "CAT5" cable)
   long enough to reach between your computer and the
   Ethernet jack located on a nearby wired/wireless router or
   on a nearby wall (such as in your office, hotel room, and so
   forth).

2. Connect one end of the Ethernet cable to the Ethernet
   port on your PC (see Figure 10-1), and then connect the
   other end to the Ethernet jack on the router or wall (see
   Figure 10-2).

Figure 10-1: Connecting Ethernet cable to PC Ethernet port

3. If you are using Windows XP, a message should appear
   near the bottom of your screen indicating that a network
   connection has been made.

Figure 10-2: Connecting Ethernet cable to Ethernet jack

Solve Problems Connecting to a Wired Network

If your computer is having difficulty connecting to a wired network, you should find out whether your network card has malfunctioned. To do so, follow these steps:

1. Click the Start button in the lower-left corner of Windows.

2. Click the Control Panel. (If you don't see this option, your Start menu is in classic mode. In that case, click Settings, and then select the Control Panel.)

3. If the Control Panel is in category view, click the Performance and Maintenance category, and then click the System icon. If the Control Panel is in classic view, simply double-click the System icon.

4. A window opens. Click the Hardware tab.

5. Click the Device Manager button.

6. The Device Manager window opens. Click the plus sign (+) next to the Network Adapters category.

7. Double-click the name of your network card.

8. Another window opens. On the General tab, look for the Device status heading. There you should see a message indicating whether or not your network card is working properly.

9. If the message says your network card is operating correctly, check to see if your connection problems have occurred because your Ethernet cable is loose or unplugged from either the network card or the Ethernet jack. Also, check for cuts, splits, or large dents on the Ethernet cable. If it is damaged, replace it, and then try your Internet connection again

10. If the message says your network card is not working properly or has an error, return to the Device Manager's main window.

11. Right-click the name of your network card, and then select Uninstall. If a message warns you that you are about to uninstall the card, click OK. This will cause your card to be uninstalled from Windows.

12. Shut down your computer and restart it. When Windows loads, it detects your network card and goes through the process of reinstalling it. If Windows cannot find the proper "drivers" to complete the setup of your card, you may have to use the installation CD that came with the card or with your computer.

13. If your connection problems continue, replace your network card.

Access the Internet from a Wireless Network

If your computer is equipped with a wireless network card (also called a Wi-Fi card), you can use it to access wireless networks at your home, office, or in a public place such as a coffee shop or bookstore.

Note
These steps apply to Windows XP only.

1. Right-click the wireless icon in the lower-right corner of Windows.

2. Click View Available Wireless Networks. If you don't see any available wireless networks, go to Step 6. Otherwise, proceed to the next step.

3. Click the wireless network you want to access (see Figure 10-3).

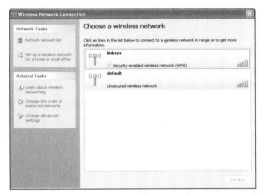

Figure 10-3: Choosing the wireless network

4. Click Connect.

5. If your version of Windows XP has Service Pack 2 installed and you are trying to access an unsecured network, you will probably have to click the Allow Me to Connect to the Selected Wireless Network Even Though It Is Not Secure option. On the other hand, if the wireless network you are connecting to is secured, you will be asked to enter an encryption key or password.

6. If you don't see any available wireless networks listed in Windows, make sure your wireless router is plugged into an electrical outlet and is working properly.

Solve Problems Connecting to a Wireless Network

If your computer is having problems accessing wireless networks, follow these fixes:

Note

These steps apply to Windows XP only.

1. Move closer to the wireless router. To have a strong connection you should be within 100 feet of the router.

2. Make sure the wireless router is plugged into an electrical outlet and appears to be turned on (as indicated by the solid or blinking lights on the front of the router).

3. Reboot your wireless router by unplugging its power cord from the electrical outlet, waiting 15 seconds, and then plugging it back in.

4. Reboot your wireless card by disabling it and then re-enabling it within Windows. Here's how:

    a. Click the Start button in the lower-left corner of Windows.

    b. Click the Control Panel. If you don't see this option, your Start menu is in classic mode. In that case, click Settings, and then select the Control Panel.

    c. If the Control Panel is in category view, click the Network and Internet Connections category, and then click the Network Connections icon. If the Control Panel is in classic view, simply double-click the Network Connections icon.

    d. Double-click the icon for your wireless connection (see Figure 10-4).

Figure 10-4: Choosing your wireless connection

    e. Wait a minute to see if a message pops up to say that the wireless card is connected to the network.

5. If the message indicates that no network connection is available, then you will have to manually set the "SSID" in the wireless card. Here's how:

   a. Double-click the wireless icon in the lower-right corner of Windows. If this icon is not available, click the Start button in the lower-left corner of Windows and click All Programs to display a list of the programs on your computer. Next, click the name of the manufacturer's configuration utility for your wireless card.

   b. After the configuration utility opens, find the section containing your wireless settings. Often, it is located on a Configuration tab.

   c. Type the name (the SSID) of the wireless network you want to access. If you do not own that network, you will need to get the SSID from the proper owner. For example, if you are trying to use a wireless network in a hotel, you will have to call the front desk and ask for its SSID.

   d. If the wireless network has encryption enabled, select the encryption type and enter the encryption key or password.

Repair a Broken Internet Connection

A common problem experienced by Windows users is a malfunctioning Internet connection. There are several reasons why this occurs — and just as many remedies.

Reboot Your Modem, Your Router, or Both

Sometimes a malfunctioning Internet connection can be caused by an error in computer hardware such as a cable/DSL modem or a router. To correct any problems with these devices, you must reboot them.

1. Shut down your computer.

2. Unplug the power cord from the back of your modem and router. An alternate method is to use the tip of a pencil to push the small "reset" button located at the rear of the modem or router.

3. The lights on the front of your modem or router will go dark. Wait 30 seconds, and then plug the power cord back in. This will cause the lights on the front of the modem or router to begin blinking rapidly in a particular pattern. Wait for an additional 30 seconds, and then restart your computer.

Temporarily Disable Your Software Firewall

Sometimes a software firewall can experience a digital "hiccup" that interferes with the way it monitors and manages your Internet connection. Common symptoms of this problem include a suddenly slow Internet connection, web pages that stall or are unresponsive, or the complete inability to access the Internet. To determine if your firewall is the cause of your problems, you can temporarily disable it.

1. Right-click the icon for your firewall, which is usually located in the lower-right corner of Windows near the clock.

2. Select the option to Close or Disable or Shut Down.

3. Try connecting to the Internet. If you are successful, restart your firewall by right-clicking its icon near the Windows clock and selecting Enable or Restore. If the firewall's icon is not there, you must manually restart the program by doing the following:

    a. Click the Start button in the lower-left corner of Windows.

    b. Click All Programs.

    c. Select the folder containing the name of your firewall software.

    d. Click the shortcut to launch the program.

4. If re-enabling your firewall causes your Internet connection to malfunction again, it is likely that your firewall has become corrupted and must be reinstalled by following the steps that follow. This requires its original installation CD-ROM or its digital installer and license key.

    a. Click the Start button in the lower-left corner of Windows.

    b. Click the Control Panel. (If you don't see this option, your Start menu is in classic mode. In that case, click Settings, and then select the Control Panel.)

   c. Double-click Add or Remove Programs.

   d. A window opens. Scroll down the list until you see the name of your firewall.

   e. Click the name of your firewall, and then click the Remove button on its right. If a message pops up and asks you if you want to uninstall the program, click Yes.

   f. After the firewall has been successfully removed, reinstall it by using its CD-ROM or installer program.

Automatically Obtain an IP Address

Another potential cause of your Internet woes may be that Windows is using an incorrect IP address. To configure Windows to automatically obtain a valid IP address, do the following:

1. Click the Start button in the lower-left corner of Windows.

2. Click the Control Panel. If you don't see this option, your Start menu is in classic mode. In that case, click Settings, and then select the Control Panel.

3. If the Control Panel is in category view, click the Network and Internet Connections category, and then click the Network Connections icon. If the Control Panel is in classic view, simply double-click the Network Connections icon.

4. Double-click the icon for your network connection.

5. A window opens. Under the tab labeled General, click the Properties button.

6. Another window opens. Click once on the words Internet Protocol (TCP/IP). Be careful not to accidentally remove the checkmark from the box.

7. Click the Properties button.

8. A new window opens. Click the Obtain an IP Address Automatically option (see Figure 10-5).

9. Click OK to save your changes.

Figure 10-5: Configuring an automatic IP address

Set a Permanent IP Address

Some Internet providers require their customers to use a static, unchanging IP address. If this is the case with your provider and you haven't configured Windows to use only one IP address, follow these steps:

1. Click the Start button in the lower-left corner of Windows.

2. Click the Control Panel. If you don't see this option, your Start menu is in classic mode. In that case, click Settings, and then select the Control Panel.

3. If the Control Panel is in category view, click the Network and Internet Connections category, and then click the Network Connections icon. If the Control Panel is in classic view, simply double-click the Network Connections icon.

4. Double-click the icon for your network connection.

5. A window opens. Under the tab labeled General, click the Properties button.

6. Another window opens. Click once on the words Internet Protocol (TCP/IP). Be careful not to remove the check-mark from the box.

7. Click the Properties button.

8. A new window opens. Click the Use the Following IP Address option (see Figure 10-6).

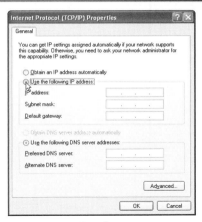

Figure 10-6: Configuring a permanent IP address

9. In the IP address box, type the numbers for the IP address given to you by your Internet provider. For example, if you were told that your permanent IP address is 192.168.1.5, you type those numbers into the box.

10. In the Subnet Mask box, type the numbers for the subnet mask given to you by your Internet provider (often those numbers will be 255.255.255.0).

11. In the Default Gateway box, type the numbers for the default gateway given to you by your Internet provider.

12. Click OK to save your changes. You may need to reboot your computer before the changes can be applied.

11

PLANNING A WIRELESS NETWORK INSTALLATION

After using CA's Desktop DNA Migrator to transfer files to a new computer, you should consider using a wireless network to make connections to the Internet easier. Before embarking on the installation of a wireless network, however, you should do your homework by thinking about what you need and the issues you might run into. Get off on the right foot by looking through this chapter and answering your initial questions before plopping down money on equipment.

There are many reasons why people use wired or wireless computer networks:

- **Share an Internet connection:** With a network, several people in your home or office can use the same high-speed Internet connection at the same time. For example, you may be researching your next vacation spot while your daughter is sending instant messages to her boyfriend.

- **Share files:** If you are tired of using floppies and USB thumbdrives to transfer files from one computer to the other, a network will make life much easier. After connecting to a network, you can simply drag and drop files from one computer to the other. After doing this a few times, you'll wonder how you ever made it through the day without a network.

- **Share a printer:** With a network, everyone can print to the same printer. For example, if you have a printer attached to a PC in your family room, you could print to it from your laptop while lounging on a hammock in the backyard. You can even attach a printer directly to the network, which will prevent someone who is printing a large document from slowing down the computer where the printer is attached.

- **Enjoy multiplayer games:** A network allows the use of interactive games, with each player sitting in front of his or her own computer. Many of the computer games on the market today have features that enable multiple players to take part in the action (assuming their computers can connect to a network). So, if you're into computer games and you have others who want to play, then don't wait. Install a network, now!

Why Go Wireless?

If you decide a network is right for you, then your next step is to select which kind you want: a traditional wired network (Ethernet) or a wireless network. Wireless, also called Wi-Fi, is rapidly growing in popularity. You have probably seen television commercials and other advertisements touting the benefits of wireless networks, or you may have friends and family who installed one. The following sections describe the advantages and disadvantages of wireless networks that you should consider when deciding if a wireless network is right for you.

Advantages of Wireless Networks

A wireless network provides the following advantages:

- **Mobility:** Similar to a cell phone, a wireless laptop or handheld computer (see Figure 11-1) enables you to communicate from just about anywhere. You're not forced to sit in front of a single desktop computer at a single location. Instead, you can use a wireless device to check your stocks while relaxing in front of the television (see Figure 11-2), check email while cooking (see Figure 11-3), or find someplace quiet in the house to get some real work done. In addition, you can take your wireless computer on the road and access the Internet from public Wi-Fi hotspots such as airports, hotels, universities, restaurants, and coffee shops.

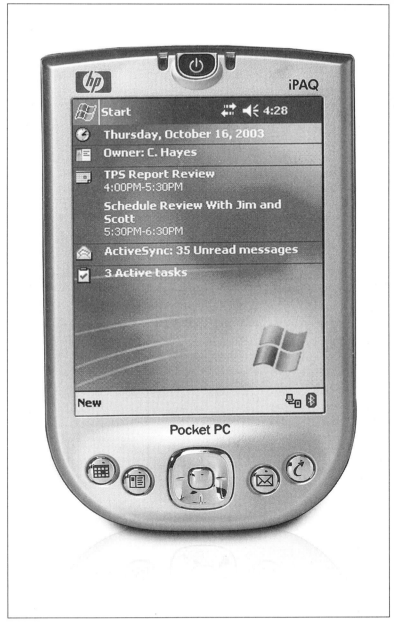

Figure 11-1: Typical handheld computer

Figure 11-2: Using a wireless network on the couch

- **Easier installation:** A wireless network doesn't require you to run massive lengths of cable between two computers (which often requires you to spend hours fishing that cable between walls and ceilings).

- **Wide coverage area:** A wireless network's signal can cover a large amount of space. For example, if you have a photography studio in your garage, you can use a wireless network to connect to a computer in your house and share an Internet account.

Note

Because wireless networks use radio waves, you may be concerned about health issues. Fortunately, research shows that the output power of wireless networks is much lower than cell phones, and there are no official reports of wireless networks causing any medical problems. However, as a precaution, you shouldn't touch the antenna of a wireless card or router while they are being used.

Figure 11-3: Using a wireless network in the kitchen

How Wireless Works

If you are installing your own wireless network, it is helpful to understand the big picture. Even if you're not technologically inclined, understanding the basic workings of your wireless network will provide you with some common sense in case you run into any problems. Here are some components and concepts you need to know:

- **Wireless card:** Each computer on the network must have a wireless card correctly installed and configured in order to send and receive wireless signals. These cards are easy to install and configure (as you will learn in Chapter 13).

- **Wireless router:** A wireless router is the main hardware in a wireless network. It links with a broadband modem to provide the network with a high-speed Internet connection. The router also sends radio signals that enable computers with wireless cards to connect to your network.

- **Medium access:** The wireless cards take turns sending data to and from each other over the air waves. Before a wireless card can transmit data, it must first analyze the air and determine whether another wireless card is transmitting a signal. If there is no signal present, the wireless card can send data. If it detects a signal, the card waits and sends the data later. This "listen-before-transmit" method regulates access to the air and only allows one wireless card to send data at any given time.

- **Traffic flow:** In most networks, the digital traffic going from one wireless computer to another passes through a wireless router. For example, when Sierra sends a digital music file from her computer to Madison's computer, her computer transmits the file to the wireless router, and then the router sends it along to Madison's computer. Figure 11-4 shows a simple diagram of the way data flows across a network.

- **"Ad hoc" wireless network:** This type of network allows computers to communicate wirelessly with each other without using a router. You can swap files anywhere without having to connect to a wireless router (see Figure 11-5).

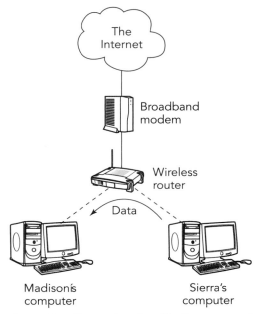

Figure 11-4: Example of traffic flow on a wireless network

Figure 11-5: Computer users on an ad hoc wireless network

Got Wireless?

Most older computers do not have wireless cards, so those cards must be purchased separately. However, if your computer is relatively new, it might already have a wireless card installed. You can find out via Windows or, if that doesn't work, you can look at your hardware, as described in the following sections.

Look Inside Windows

Follow these steps to use Windows to see if you have a wireless card:

1. Right-click the My Computer icon on your desktop. If this icon is not available, click the Start button in the lower-left corner of Windows and click My Computer. If you can't find the My Computer icon anywhere, do the following:

   a. Right-click in the empty space on your desktop.

   b. Select Properties.

   c. A window opens. Click the Desktop tab.

   d. Near the bottom of the window, click the Customize Desktop button.

   e. Another window opens. On the General tab, beneath Desktop Icons, place a checkmark in the My Computer box.

   f. Click the OK button.

   g. You will be returned to the previous screen. Click the Apply button.

   h. Click the OK button.

   i. The My Computer icon appears on your desktop. Right-click it.

2. Select Properties.

3. A window opens. Click the Hardware tab.

4. Click the Device Manager button.

5. Click the + (plus sign) located next to the Network Adapters category. If there are icons under Network Adapters, you need to figure out what type they are. An Ethernet card (used with a traditional, wired network) has

a label that says something like 10/100 or Ethernet. If the label mentions the word "wireless" — such as "wireless PCI card" — then it is a wireless card. Figure 11-6 shows a wireless card in the Device Manager.

Figure 11-6: Wireless card in Device Manager

If you cannot find the Network Adapters category or if no icons appear under this category when you click the +, then most likely you do not have a wireless card installed. To be sure, you should look at your computer's hardware.

Look at Your Hardware

If you have looked in Windows but still can't determine whether you have a wireless card installed, you should inspect your computer's hardware.

If you have a laptop computer:

- There is no quick way to determine whether you have an *internal* wireless card. Both the card and antenna are mounted inside your laptop behind an access door. In some cases, your laptop may have a manufacturer's label that indicates an internal wireless card exists.

- If you have an external wireless card, it sticks out of a slot on the side of your laptop (see Figure 11-7).

Figure 11-7: Typical external wireless card in laptop

Follow these steps if you have a desktop computer:

1. Move your computer's case so you can see its back. Be careful not to yank out or disconnect any wires.

2. If you have a wireless card installed, an antenna several inches long extends from the back of the computer. This antenna is attached to a card mounted inside the computer's case (see Figure 11-8).

3. Some wireless cards have desktop antennas connected to them. You can check for this by following any wires coming from your computer's cards.

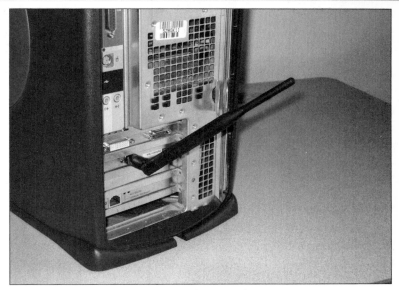

Figure 11-8: Typical desktop wireless card

The Lowdown on Wi-Fi

Wireless Fidelity (Wi-Fi) is a brand name given to wireless networks by the Wi-Fi Alliance (an organization that governs Wi-Fi products). There are several versions of Wi-Fi: 802.11a, 802.11b, and 802.11g, each of which uses different methods for transmitting and receiving data. For more information about their differences, see Table 1-1.

Table 1-1: Wi-Fi Standards

Technology	Frequency Band	Speed	Uses
802.11b	2.4 GHz	Up to 11 Mbps	Ideal for older wireless networks
802.11g	2.4 GHz	Up to 54 Mbps	Great for email and web browsing
802.11g with SpeedBooster	2.4 GHz	Up to 108 Mbps	Enables faster file downloads
802.11a	5 GHz	Up to 54 Mbps	Delivers higher performance when significant radio-frequency interference is present

It is important to understand that the 802.11b and 802.11g technologies are compatible with each other, so even if you have older 802.11b equipment, it still works with the newer 802.11g equipment. Also, be aware that in order to use the 802.11g "SpeedBooster" feature, both your wireless router and wireless card must support it.

Note
The number 802.11 comes from the group that developed the initial standards for local area networks. The 80 refers to the year they began their work—1980—and the 2 refers to the actual month they began—February, the second month. The 11 was later given to the 802 group that created the wireless LAN standard because it was the eleventh standard they had developed.

Ensure Compatibility
Because there are several different standards of wireless networks, you must buy a wireless card that is compatible with your wireless router. Otherwise, the devices won't be able to "talk" to each other. In addition, if you are planning to use special features like SpeedBooster or power saving, you must make sure those features are properly set up. Here are some general guidelines for ensuring compatibility:

- **Use compatible technologies:** Make sure the wireless card and wireless router are using the same frequency. For example, a 2.4 GHz wireless card (802.11b or 802.11g) can only connect to a 2.4 GHz wireless router (802.11b or 802.11g). It cannot connect to a 5 GHz (802.11a) wireless router.

Note
If you want wireless equipment that can work with any 802.11 standard (a, b, or g), buy a "dual-band" router and card.

- **Buy Wi-Fi certified hardware:** Look for the Wi-Fi certification listed on the product packaging or on the product itself. You can also visit the Wi-Fi Alliance's website (www.wi-fi.com) to view the products that have Wi-Fi certification.

- **Use the same manufacturer:** If possible, use the same brand of wireless cards and routers. This allows you to take advantage of special manufacturer-specific enhancements, such as SpeedBooster or range-extension techniques.

Increase the Lifespan of Your Wireless Equipment

As with any other computer technology, wireless networks have rapidly evolved, becoming faster and more secure. Newer wireless equipment should last for many years until something better comes along that is more appealing. Here are a few tips to keep your wireless equipment from becoming outdated too soon:

- **Buy Wi-Fi certified equipment:** This can't be said enough. If you don't purchase devices that have an official Wi-Fi certification, you run the risk of having that equipment become troublesome or unusable in the near future.

- **Check for firmware and driver updates:** Periodically, hardware manufacturers release two kinds of updates for their equipment: firmware and drivers. These updates fix problems, offer enhanced features, and plug security holes. It is a good idea to check for new firmware and drivers every few months just to stay safe. Some manufacturers send email announcements to inform you when updates are available, but others require you to check their website.

The Equipment You'll Need for a Network

To set up a wireless network, you need to learn some high-tech terminology and purchase special equipment.

Untangle the Terminology

Whether you're browsing the shelves in a computer store or researching Wi-Fi products on the Internet, you might be confused by the high-tech lingo. Often there are several names that mean the same thing, so here is a quick rundown of common Wi-Fi words and their synonyms:

- **Wireless router:** Also called a wireless broadband router or an access point.

- **Wireless card:** Also called a PCI adapter, desktop adapter, Wi-Fi adapter, or wireless adapter.

- **Notebook adapter:** Also called a cardbus adapter, wireless PC card, radio card, Wi-Fi adapter, or wireless adapter.

- **2.4 GHz:** Also called 802.11b, 802.11g, b, or g.

- **5 GHz:** Also called 802.11a, Wi-Fi5, or a.

Wireless Router

The average wireless router (as shown in Figure 11-9) has a range of 100 feet, so if you are interested in setting up a wireless network in your home or small office, you should only need one router. Some routers are "single-band" and implement either 2.4 GHz technologies (802.11b and 802.11g) or 5 GHz technologies (802.11a). Some routers, though, are "dual-band," which means they use both 2.4 GHz and 5 GHz frequencies. Consider the following when deciding whether to purchase a dual-band router:

- **Price:** The price of dual-band routers is generally 25 percent higher than a standalone 2.4 GHz (802.11g) router.

- **Compatibility:** Because the majority of laptops and PCs come equipped with a 2.4 GHz (802.11b or 802.11g) wireless card, you can probably get by with only having an 802.11g router. Don't forget, a 2.4 GHz wireless card can't connect to a 5 GHz router, so no matter what type you choose, always use wireless equipment that shares the same frequency.

- **Performance:** There is much less interference in the 5 GHz band, which means that 802.11a routers can operate with fewer interruptions than 802.11g routers.

Figure 11-9: Typical wireless router

Wireless Card

There are several types of wireless cards to choose from:

- **PCI card:** You'll need a wireless PCI card for each computer you want to connect to a wireless network. The card shown in Figure 11-10 inserts into your computer.

- **Notebook adapters:** You need a wireless notebook card (see Figure 11-11) for each laptop or handheld computer. Before spending money on equipment, make sure your handheld computer has a notebook adapter slot. Usually this slot is located on the top of the computer. Also, look in your owner's manual to verify whether your handheld computer will accommodate a notebook adapter.

Figure 11-10: Typical wireless PCI card

Figure 11-11: Typical notebook wireless card

- **Compact Flash adapter:** You may need a wireless Compact Flash (CF) adapter for each handheld computer you want to connect to a wireless network (see Figure 11-12). Before spending money on equipment, make sure your handheld computer has a CF adapter slot. Usually this slot is located on the top of the computer. Also, look in your owner's manual to verify whether your handheld computer will accommodate a CF card.

Figure 11-12: Typical compact flash adapter

- **USB adapters:** Use this type if you have an available USB port and want to avoid the hassles of opening up your desktop computer and inserting a card.

- **Antenna:** In most cases you can use the antenna that came with your wireless card. However, if the antenna is removable, you can purchase a replacement that is more powerful.

Determine the Number of Cards You Need

Here are some things to consider when deciding how many wireless cards you should purchase:

- Buy one wireless card for each computer you want to connect to the network.

- You can save money by using an inexpensive Ethernet cable to connect your desktop or laptop computer to the traditional wired ports on the back of the wireless router.

Add Bells and Whistles

To boost the performance of your wireless network, there are a few enhancements you can use, as described in the following sections.

MIMO

MIMO (which stands for multiple input, multiple output) is a feature appearing in new routers that enables you to improve the performance of your wireless signal by using "smart" antennas. Here are some things to consider about MIMO:

- **Standards:** Currently there are no official standards for MIMO. It is being incorporated into a new wireless standard called 802.11n, but the approval process has been slow. As a result, the standard may not become available until 2007. Some manufacturers have already produced MIMO-based wireless routers, but these are unofficial.

- **Do you need MIMO?** The answer is probably no, especially if your home or office can get by with a single router without MIMO. Routers with MIMO cost more, so if you don't need it, don't buy it.

SpeedBooster

Some wireless hardware has an enhancement known as "SpeedBooster" that doubles its speed. For example, it can increase the data rate of an 802.11g router from 54 Mbps to 108 Mbps. If you purchase a wireless product with this feature, consider the following tips:

- **Use the same brand of equipment:** Because SpeedBooster is not an official Wi-Fi standard, you have to use wireless cards and routers from the same manufacturer.

- **Enable it on all equipment:** If you want to take advantage of SpeedBooster, you must turn on this feature in the wireless router and in each wireless card.

Upgrade the Antenna

In most cases, you can use the antenna that came with your wireless router. However, if the antenna is removable, you can replace it with one that is stronger and has a better range. Here are some general guidelines:

- **Visit the manufacturer's website:** By researching the styles of antennas offered by the manufacturer of your wireless router, you will be able to buy one that properly fits your router. Don't forget: you can't replace an antenna that isn't removable.

- **Purchase from a third party:** You can purchase a variety of antennas for Wi-Fi devices from third party vendors.

- **Check for compatibility:** When you order antennas, be sure they are designed to work with your brand of wireless equipment. Different manufacturers use different types of antenna connectors, so it is important to get this right. Otherwise, you won't be able to attach the new antenna to your device.

Note

Some replacement antennas come with several different connectors, so be sure to read the instructions to know which connector to use with your particular wireless card or router.

Hardware and Software Requirements

Wireless cards are designed to work with a variety of operating systems, such as Windows, Mac OS, and Linux. The memory and processor speeds are minimal, so it is unlikely you will encounter any issues with compatibility. Here are some tips to consider:

- **Use Windows XP:** The most recent version of Windows, known as Windows XP, makes it easy to set up and use wireless networks. If you don't have XP, you can buy a copy and perform a manual upgrade or you can have an onsite service technician come to your home or office to do the upgrade.

- **Have a CD drive available:** Make sure your computer has a CD-ROM drive, because you probably need to install software for your wireless router or card that comes on a CD-ROM.

Estimate Your Network's Cost

Here are some approximate prices for the devices you must purchase to set up a wireless network:

- **Wireless adapter:** $20 to $80
- **Wireless router:** $30 to $100

Note

Prices vary depending on the features you choose. For example, a wireless router that uses MIMO technology to improve performance may cost 50 percent more than a router without MIMO. Also, keep in mind that the prices of most wireless network components have been steadily decreasing in recent years and will likely continue to do so.

Which Manufacturer Is Best?

Several major companies produce outstanding wireless network products for homes and small businesses. To pick the best brand of wireless products for your needs, consider the following:

- **Price.** When shopping around to get the lowest possible price on wireless equipment, keep in mind that cheaper is not always better. Don't go with no-name brands just to save a few bucks. Stick with a reputable manufacturer's products.

- **Enhancements.** Look for special features like MIMO and SpeedBooster. Investigate whether the manufacturer also sells wireless companion products such as digital media players, cameras, and print servers. If so, your network has room to grow and won't have problems connecting to those other products.

- **User friendliness.** Look at the packaging to see if there are any clues about how easy the product will be to install. However, don't base your entire decision on the package.

Note

If you already know what wireless products you want to buy, consider purchasing them from an Internet store. Often this can save you quite a bit of money.

The Effects of Bad Weather

Heavy rain, fog, and other undesirable weather conditions decrease the range of some wireless networks, such as those providing wireless connections between buildings in a city. But for small wireless networks less than 500 feet in diameter—like the kind found in the average home or office—the impact of bad weather is undetectable.

How Many Computers Does a Network Support?

The average wireless router can support up to 20 wireless computers. However, using an Internet telephone (referred to as voice over IP, or VoIP for short) may strain the network and make it feel sluggish. If this happens, consider using two or more routers in the same area, but set them to different channels.

12

SETTING UP A
WIRELESS NETWORK

I f after using CA's Desktop DNA Migrator to transfer files to a new computer you decide to connect
your new PC to the Internet wirelessly, then read
through this chapter to understand the ins and outs of
setting up a wireless network. It will save you a great
deal of time!

The purchase, installation, and configuration of your
new wireless network can take several hours. Before
investing all of that time (and money), read through
this general overview of the steps involved:

1. Find a location in your home or office to set
   up the wireless router. This may require some
   trial and error to find the optimum spot.

2. Install and configure your wireless router.

3. Install and configure a wireless card in each
   computer.

4. After you finish the installation, check to
   make sure that each computer can connect to
   the router and can browse the Internet.

5. Install and configure any optional wireless
   components. For example, you may want
   to install a wireless print server, video game
   adapter, digital media player, or webcam.

Find the Best Place to Install Your Router

One of the most important steps in setting up a wireless network is to place the router in a location that gives you the best possible wireless access and coverage. Before picking a spot, think about the areas in your home or office where you will frequently use your wireless or wired computers and mobile devices. Here are some tips for finding a good location:

- **Install near the broadband modem:** If you are planning to share an Internet connection with two or more computers, you should install your wireless router near the DSL, satellite, or cable modem. Doing so will allow you to easily run a cable between the modem and the router. If this location doesn't provide adequate wireless coverage, you can move your modem to a different wall outlet (in which case you may need the services of a computer professional).

- **Install near the center of your coverage area:** After deciding the general area of your home or office where you want to have a wireless network, you should install the wireless router in the center of that area. This will ensure that your wireless computers and mobile devices have access to strong wireless signals no matter where you go in your coverage area.

Types of Wireless Networks

There are three types of wireless networks: a wireless router connected to high-speed Internet, an ad hoc network, and a partially wired network.

Wireless Router Connected to High-Speed Internet

The most common type of wireless network uses a wireless router to regulate the flow of information and connect you to a traditional wired network (like the Internet). See Figure 12-1 for a diagram of a network that has a router connected to high-speed Internet.

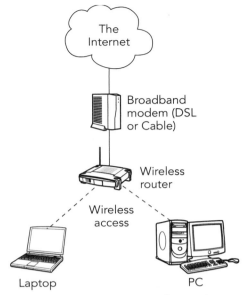

Figure 12-1: Typical setup of a wireless network

Here are common reasons why you might choose this type of network:

- You need to connect your computer to the Internet.
- You want to share an Internet connection with multiple computers.
- You want to access public wireless networks.

Connect the Router to a Broadband Modem

Here is a general overview of the steps required to connect a router to a high-speed Internet connection (also known as a broadband connection):

1. Sign up for Internet access with a broadband service provider, such as cable, satellite, or DSL. Your service company installs a broadband outlet in your home or office and likely connects a modem (see Figure 12-2) to this outlet. If you don't receive a broadband modem as part of your subscription, you need to rent or purchase one. Check with your service provider for information on obtaining a compatible modem.

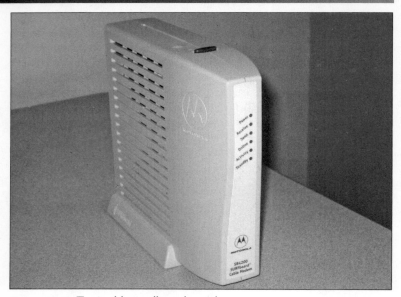

Figure 12-2: Typical broadband modem

2. If your service provider didn't connect the modem, you need to connect it to the wall outlet by using the Category 5 Ethernet cable (often called a CAT5 cable) supplied by your provider. Generally they are gray, yellow, or blue in color and resemble a large telephone cord (see Figure 12-3). If a CAT5 cable didn't come bundled with your router or modem, you must purchase one from a computer or electronics store.

3. Plug one end of the CAT5 cable into the slot on the router labeled "WAN" or "Internet." You will know the cable has been inserted properly when you hear it snap into place.

4. Plug the other end of the CAT5 cable into the slot on the broadband modem labeled "LAN" or "Network." You will know the cable has been inserted properly when you hear it snap into place.

Note

The slots on the back of some broadband modems do not have labels like WAN or Internet. In that case, find the slot that looks like it will connect to a large telephone cord. That is where you should plug your CAT5 cable.

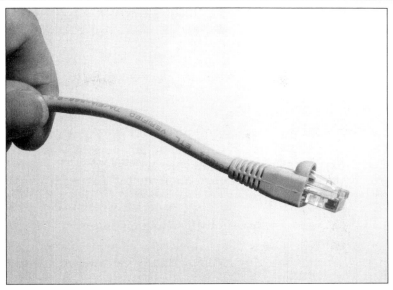

Figure 12-3: Ethernet (CAT5) cabling

An Ad Hoc Network

Another type of wireless network known as "ad hoc" (also called "peer-to-peer") allows computers to communicate wirelessly with each other without using a router (see Figure 12-4).

Wireless laptops

Figure 12-4: Example of a wireless peer-to-peer network

You might consider using this type of network if . . .

- There aren't any wireless routers installed at your location but you want to transfer a file from one wireless computer to another.

- You don't need to connect to the Internet.

- You are away from your home or office but want to use a network to swap files, share printers, or play multiplayer video games.

The following sections describe the methods for setting up an ad hoc network.

Use the Manufacturer's Configuration Utility

The most common way to set up an ad hoc network is to use the special software that comes with your wireless card. This software is usually referred to as a "configuration utility." To use a configuration utility, follow these steps:

1. Access your wireless card's configuration utility.

   a. Usually this can be done by double-clicking the configuration utility's icon located in the lower-right corner of Windows.

   b. If you don't see it, click the Start menu in the lower-left corner of Windows, click All Programs, and then select the configuration utility that corresponds to the name of your wireless card.

2. Once you have successfully accessed the configuration utility, look for the SSID feature. This is the name of your ad hoc network. You should change the name to one of your choosing (feel free to be creative).

Note

For enhanced security, use a combination of letters and numbers. Also, don't forget that an SSID is case sensitive, which means it considers uppercase and lowercase letters to be different.

3. Choose a channel for your ad hoc network. Usually it doesn't matter which channel you select, but try to pick one that is different from those being used by nearby routers (this will reduce the possibility of interference from the other routers).

4. Change the wireless mode to Ad Hoc (or, in some cases, you may have to select Peer-to-Peer).

5. Click Apply to save the changes.

Use Windows XP's Configuration Utility

Another way to set up an ad hoc network is to use the built-in features of Windows XP, as follows:

1. Right-click the wireless icon located in the lower-right corner of Windows (see Figure 12-5).

Figure 12-5: Accessing wireless menu

2. Click View Available Wireless Networks.

3. If your version of Windows XP has Service Pack 2 installed, click the Change Advanced Settings option. If you don't have Service Pack 2, click the Advanced option (see Figure 12-6).

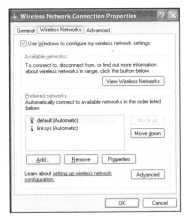

Figure 12-6: Wireless Network Connection Properties

4. Click the Wireless Networks tab.

5. Click Add.

6. In the Network Name (SSID box), type a new name for your ad hoc network. You can create any name you want, so feel free to be creative.

Note

For enhanced security, use a combination of letters and numbers. Also, don't forget that an SSID is case sensitive, which means it considers uppercase and lowercase letters to be different.

7. Near the bottom of the window, put a checkmark in the box labeled "This is a computer-to-computer (ad-hoc) network; wireless access points are not used" (see Figure 12-7).

Figure 12-7: Enabling peer-to-peer mode

8. To protect your ad hoc network from hackers, you should turn on its encryption features, as follows:

   a. Click the Data Encryption drop-down menu.

   b. Select an encryption type.

   c. Type a password.

9. Click the OK button. The wireless card starts operating as an ad hoc device, meaning it will not connect to any routers. As a result, you cannot use the Internet unless you set up Internet-sharing on one of the computers.

Note

Other people can easily connect their computers to your ad hoc network. First, they must access their wireless card's configuration utility, select the Display option, and connect to ad hoc networks. Next, they should right-click the wireless icon located in the lower-right corner of Windows and select the View Available Wireless Networks option. Finally, they must select the SSID name you created for your ad hoc network.

A Partially Wired Network

On the back of most wireless routers are Ethernet connections identical to those found on a traditional wired router. This allows the wireless router to share files and an Internet connection with computers that don't have wireless cards. This setup is known as a "partially wired network" (see Figure 12-8).

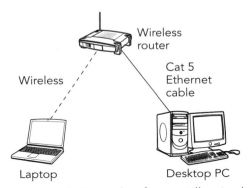

Figure 12-8: Example of a partially wired network

Note

If there aren't enough ports available on the wireless router, you can connect the router to an Ethernet hub.

Set Up a Partially Wired Network

Assembling a partially wired network is easier than it may seem. Just follow these steps:

1. Make sure your computer has an Ethernet card. To do so, look for an opening in the back of the computer that seems like it could connect to a large telephone cord. This opening might be labeled "Data," "Ethernet," or "RJ-45."

2. Obtain a CAT5 cable long enough to reach from the computer to the wireless router.

3. On the back of most routers are Ethernet ports numbered from 1 through 4. Plug the CAT5 cable into any of these ports by snapping the connector into place (see Figure 12-9).

4. Connect the other end of the cable to one of the Ethernet ports on the wireless router.

Note

The CAT5 cable must be less than 300 feet long.

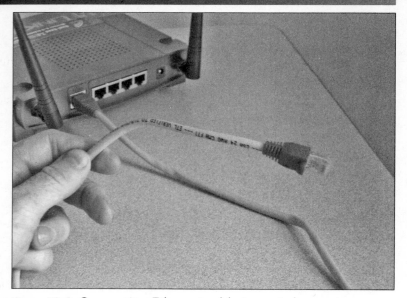

Figure 12-9: Connecting Ethernet cable to a wireless router

Connect a Wireless Router to an Existing Wired Network

Even if you already have a traditional wired network, you can easily
add a wireless network. Doing so will enable you to share files and
an Internet connection with mobile computers or other mobile
devices you may purchase in the near future (see Figure 12-10).

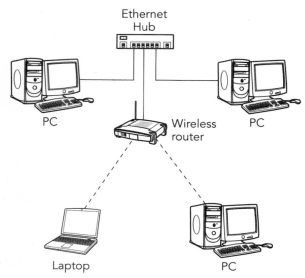

Figure 12-10: Depiction of a wireless router connected to a
wired network

1. Plug a CAT5 cable into the LAN port on your wireless router.

2. Connect the other end of the cable to a hub or wired router on your existing wired network.

3. Install and configure the wireless router, following the manufacturer's installation guide.

High-Tech Fun in the Sun

Have you ever thought about how much fun it would be to surf the web while relaxing in a hammock in your backyard or lounging by your pool? With wireless networks, it's possible. If you have tried to extend the range of your indoor wireless network but it won't reach outdoors, you will probably need to install a router outside. This can take some effort, so be sure you really want wireless coverage outside before going any further. Figure 12-11 shows you how an exterior router can connect to a wireless network you already have installed inside your home or office.

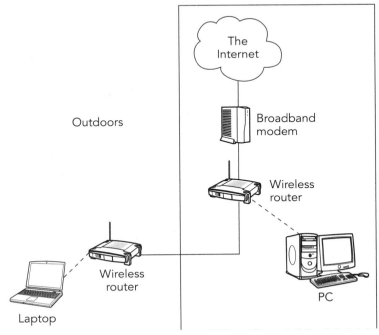

Figure 12-11: Example of extending a wireless network outdoors

Install a Wireless Router Outdoors

Here are the basic steps you must take to install a wireless router outside:

1. Obtain a wireless router rated for outdoor installations, or use a regular interior wireless router in combination with a special weatherproof enclosure recommended by the router's manufacturer. Usually these enclosures aren't available at the average computer or electronics store, so you will probably need to purchase one on the Internet, either from the manufacturer's website or from an Internet store.

2. Find a good exterior location that will prevent large amounts of rain and snow from hitting the router, such as underneath the edge of your roof.

3. Mount the router. Most exterior routers come with plenty of mounting brackets.

4. Connect the exterior router to your existing interior wireless network, as follows:

   a. Purchase a CAT5 cable long enough to stretch from the exterior router to the interior router.

   b. Run the cable from the exterior router to the interior router. This may require you to drill holes in the side of your house and fish the cable through walls.

   c. Plug one end of the cable into an available Ethernet port on the exterior router, and then plug the other end of the cable into an available Ethernet port on the interior router.

   d. Power up the exterior router. If the Ethernet cable doesn't supply electricity to the router (which is called "power-over-Ethernet"), use an extension cord to plug the exterior router into an exterior electrical outlet.

5. Configure the router. Be sure to do the following:

   a. Change the name of your exterior router (its SSID) to match the SSID of the interior router. This allows you to roam from inside to outside without having to reconnect to both networks each time.

b. Change the channel of the exterior router so it does not use the same one as the interior router. To avoid interference, only use channels 1, 6, and 11.

c. Configure the exterior router to give it the same security settings as your interior router.

d. To avoid conflicts, disable the "DHCP" feature on the exterior router.

13

INSTALLING A
WIRELESS CARD

I f after using CA's Desktop DNA Migrator to transfer files to a new computer you decide to connect
your new PC to the Internet wirelessly, then read
through this chapter to learn the process of installing a
wireless card that enables your computer to "talk" to
the wireless router.

This chapter guides you through the process of
installing a wireless card that enables your computer
to "talk" to the wireless router. Figure 13-1 shows a
typical wireless card.

Figure 13-1: Typical wireless card for desktop PCs

Consult the User Guide

Your product's user guide contains answers to frequently answered questions, valuable information about how to access configuration screens and troubleshoot problems, and much more. When you are installing a wireless network or attempting to solve a problem with it, read the user guide first.

Most wireless network products don't come with a printed user guide, so you need to locate it on the CD-ROM that came with your hardware. In many cases, the user guide can be accessed through a window that pops up after you insert the CD. If no pop-up window appears, you can manually search for the user guide by doing the following:

1. Double-click the My Computer icon on your desktop. If this icon is not available, click the Start button in the lower-left corner of Windows and click My Computer. If you can't find the My Computer icon anywhere, do the following:

    a. Right-click in the empty space on your desktop.

    b. Select Properties.

    c. A window opens. Click the Desktop tab.

d. Click the Customize Desktop button near the bottom of the window.

e. Another window opens. On the General tab, beneath Desktop Icons, place a checkmark in the My Computer box.

f. Click the OK button.

g. You are returned to the previous screen. Click the Apply button.

h. Click the OK button.

i. The My Computer icon appears on your desktop. Double-click it.

2. Right-click the icon for your CD or DVD drive, and then click Explore.

3. The user guide is often found in a folder on the Docs or Manual CD. The name of the user guide usually contains the model number for your product.

4. If you can't find your product's CD, you can usually download the user guide from the Support section of the manufacturer's website. Make sure you know the model number of your product in order to download the correct manual.

Note
User guides typically come in PDF format, which requires the Adobe Acrobat Reader to view them. If this software isn't installed on your computer, check the setup CD that came with your wireless product to see if a copy is included. If not, you can download Acrobat Reader free of charge at http://www.adobe.com.

Install a Wireless Card in a Desktop Computer

When installing a wireless card in a desktop computer, always follow the instructions that came with the card. Here is a general overview of the steps involved:

1. **Follow the proper instructions:** Most user guides include different instructions for different versions of Windows (such as Windows XP or Windows 98), so be sure to follow the set of instructions that were designed for your version of Windows.

2. **Turn off the computer and unplug it:** To protect yourself from being shocked or damaging the computer's components, you must shut down Windows, turn off the
   computer, and unplug it from all electrical outlets.

3. **Open the computer's case:** Almost every desktop computer allows you to open its case for the purpose of accessing or changing its components. Depending on how your
   desktop computer was built, the whole case may slide open,
   one side may slide open, or one side may swing open like a
   door.

4. **Insert the wireless card:** After opening the computer's
   case, look for an empty PCI slot on the motherboard where
   you can insert the wireless card. See Figure 13-2 to get an
   idea of what a PCI slot looks like. Before inserting the card,
   you will probably need to remove a small metal cover
   located adjacent to the PCI slot. This can be done by
   removing the screw that holds the cover in place. Again,
   refer to Figure 13-2 for an example of what the slot looks
   like with the cover removed. When sliding the wireless card
   into a PCI slot, make sure it snaps into place and is not
   loose. The side the card with the antenna should stick out
   the back of the computer through the open slot.

Figure 13-2: Empty PCI slot in a PC

5. Install the software and configure the card: Sometimes Windows detects and configures a wireless card without asking for additional software, but it is always a good idea to follow the instructions provided by the card's manufacturer and install the special software that came with the card. Typically this software includes updates and utilities that make the installation easier and enhance the card's performance.

Note

Read the manufacturer's instructions carefully because you may be asked to install the software before physically installing the wireless card (or vice versa).

Install a Wireless Card in a Laptop

When installing a wireless card in a laptop computer, always follow the instructions that came with the card. Here is a general overview of the steps involved:

1. Obtain a notebook wireless card: This is the only type of wireless card that will plug into your laptop. You don't have to buy the card from the same manufacturer as your wireless router, but make sure the card and the router use the same frequency (either 2.4 GHz or 5 GHz).

2. Connect a CD-ROM drive (if necessary): If the installation requires a CD-ROM to be used (which is likely), make sure you have a CD drive. Some lightweight laptops don't come with a CD drive, so you might need to use an external drive. If you don't have any type of CD drive available, you might be able to download the software for your wireless card by visiting the manufacturer's website.

3. Follow the proper instructions: Most user guides include different instructions for different versions of Windows (such as Windows XP or Windows 98), so be sure to follow the set of instructions that were designed for your version of Windows.

4. Insert the wireless card: Choose an empty slot on your laptop (you probably only have one), and then insert the card (see Figure 13-3). Although the card can only go in one way, be gentle because the card and the slot are somewhat fragile.

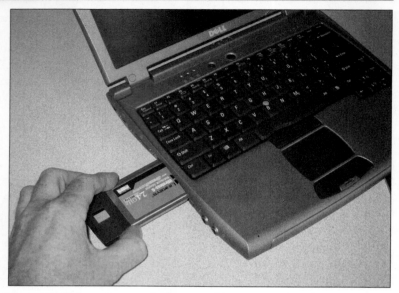

Figure 13-3: Inserting a wireless card into a notebook

5. Install the software and configure the card: Sometimes Windows detects and configures a wireless card without asking for additional software, but it is always a good idea to follow the instructions provided by the card's manufacturer and install the special software that came with the card. Typically this software includes updates and utilities that make the installation easier and enhance the card's performance.

Note

Read the manufacturer's instructions carefully because you may be asked to install the software before physically installing the wireless card (or vice versa).

Update the Drivers for Your Wireless Card

To get the best performance from your wireless card, you should update it with the most recent "drivers," which are a type of software that controls your card. Occasionally manufacturers release new drivers for their products to offer enhanced features, fix errors, and plug security holes.

Determine the Current Version

Before making changes to your drivers, you must find out what version they are.

Follow these steps to determine the version of your wireless card drivers on Windows XP Home Edition and XP Professional Edition:

1. Double-click the wireless icon located in the lower-right corner of Windows.

2. Select Properties.

3. Click Configure.

4. Click the Driver tab (see Figure 13-4).

Figure 13-4: Driver details

5. Grab a pen and paper and jot down the version number and release date for your wireless card's drivers.

Follow these steps to determine the version of your wireless card drivers on Windows 98:

1. Right-click the My Computer icon on your desktop.

2. Select Properties.

3. Click the Device Manager tab.

4. Click the + (plus sign) located next to the Network Adapters category.

5. Double-click the wireless card you want to check.

6. Click the Driver tab.

7. Click Driver File Details.

8. Grab a pen and paper and jot down the version number and release date for your wireless card's drivers.

Check for New Drivers

To determine if your drivers need to be updated, do the following:

1. Visit the website belonging to the manufacturer of your wireless card. Click the Support or Downloads section of the site, and then look for information about drivers.

2. Locate the drivers on the website that correspond to your specific brand and model of wireless card.

3. Compare the version number of your current drivers with the ones available on the website. If the website's drivers have a higher number than yours, that means your current drivers are outdated. Go ahead and download the new ones. Be sure to save them in a folder you can easily find later, because you will need to access that folder when you update the drivers in the next step.

Update the Drivers

After downloading the new drivers, you need to update your wireless card through Windows.

To update your wireless card on Windows XP Home Edition and XP Professional Edition:

1. Double-click the wireless icon located in the lower-right corner of Windows.

2. Select Properties.

3. Click Configure.

4. Click the Driver tab.

5. Click Update Driver (see Figure 13-5).

6. Follow the on-screen instructions.

Figure 13-5: Updating the driver

To update your wireless card on Windows 98:

1. Right-click the My Computer icon on your desktop.

2. Select Properties.

3. Click the Device Manager tab.

4. Click the + (plus sign) located next to the Network Adapters category.

5. Double-click the wireless card you want to update.

6. Click the Driver tab.

7. Click Update Driver.

8. Follow the on-screen instructions.

Window XP's Wireless Auto Configuration

Windows XP offers Zero Configuration and Wireless Auto Configuration services that make it easier to use wireless networks. With Wireless Auto Configuration, you don't have to fiddle with the often confusing configuration utilities that come with wireless cards. Here is how the Wireless Auto Configuration works:

1. The Wireless Auto Configuration prompts you with a message that says that wireless networks have been detected (see Figure 13-6).

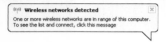

Figure 13-6: Wireless network detection prompt

2. Open the Wireless Network Connection dialog box.

3. Select the network you want to connect to (see **Figure 13-7**).

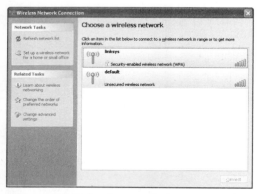

Figure 13-7: Selecting a wireless network

4. Windows attempts to connect to the network. If the network is protected with security features, you may be required to enter a WEP key or WPA key (which are similar to passwords).

One of the following occurs:

• If Windows successfully connects to the network, that network is automatically added to your list of preferred networks (see Figure 13-8).

• If Windows can't connect to any of the networks that are currently available, it tries to connect to the ones found in your list of preferred networks (previously shown in Figure 13-7). If Windows can't connect to those preferred networks, it uses your wireless card to scan for the presence of any wireless networks within range.

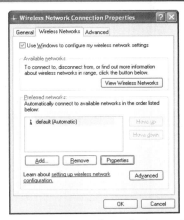

Figure 13-8: Preferred Network list

- If you are using the Windows "Automatically connect to non-preferred networks" feature (see Figure 13-9), your computer automatically connects to the first wireless network it finds. If you have disabled this feature (as in Figure 13-10), Windows does not connect to any wireless networks it finds. Instead, Windows displays a message that says, "One or more wireless networks are available" (previously shown in Figure 13-6). This gives you complete control over which wireless network your computer accesses.

Figure 13-9: Automatic Connection to Non-Preferred Networks is enabled

Figure 13-10: Automatic Connection to Non-Preferred Networks is disabled

Appendix

SUPPORTED SETTINGS

Application Settings

- ACT!
- Adobe Acrobat
- Adobe Reader
- Adobe Illustrator
- Adobe InDesign
- Adobe Pagemaker
- Adobe PageMill
- Adobe Photoshop
- Adobe Type Manager Deluxe
- America Online (AOL)
- AOL Instant Messenger
- Backup Exec Desktop Pro
- Blackberry Desktop Manager
- Corel Paradox
- Corel Presentations
- Corel Quattro Pro
- Corel WordPerfect
- Corel Central
- DataViz Conversion Plus Suite
- Eudora Pro
- Exceed
- Executive Software Diskeeper Workstation
- FileMaker Pro

- GoldMine
- HomeSite
- ICQ
- Lotus 1-2-3
- Lotus Approach
- Lotus Freelance Graphics
- Lotus Notes
- Lotus Organizer
- Lotus WordPro
- Macromedia Director
- Macromedia Dreamweaver
- Macromedia Fireworks
- Macromedia Freehand
- McAfee VirusScan
- Microsoft Access
- Microsoft Excel
- Microsoft Exchange
- Microsoft FrontPage
- Microsoft Internet Explorer
- Microsoft Meeting
- Microsoft Office Shortcut Bar
- Microsoft Outlook
- Microsoft Outlook Express
- Microsoft PowerPoint
- Microsoft Project
- Microsoft Visio
- Microsoft Word
- MSN
- MSN Messenger
- Netscape Communicator
- Netscape Navigator

- Norton Antivirus
- Norton Ghost
- Norton Internet Security
- Norton Utilities NT
- Novell Networking
- Paint Shop Pro
- Palm Desktop
- PC MacLAN
- QuarkXpress
- Quick View Plus
- QuickBooks Pro
- Quicken Deluxe
- RealOne Player
- Reflection Suite TCP
- Siebel Sales, Personal Edition
- Symantec pcAnywhere
- System Mechanic
- Timbuktu
- Winamp
- Windows Media Player
- Windows Messaging
- WinFax Pro
- WinZip

System Settings

- Command Prompt
- Data Sources (ODBC)
- Desktop Settings
  - Appearance (icons, fonts, scheme, and theme)
  - Background (pattern, wallpaper, wallpaper position)
  - Desktop Settings (keyboard configuration, languages, mouse configuration, pointer scheme)

- Screen saver (current screen saver, energy options, password, wait times)
- Arrange Icons, Desktop Clean Up Wizard, Regional Settings, Folder Options, Send To, Sounds, Taskbar
- Time Zone, Web Settings
- Multilingual User Interface
- Networking (protocol settings (TCP/IP) authentication, identification, share points)
- Printers
- Quick Launch Toolbar

Data Migration

- My Documents file and subfolders.
- You are able to select any files and folders you wish from your directory.
- You have access to a powerful filter mechanism using sophisticated methods to collect files and folders anywhere they exist on your old PC and back up or transfer them to your new PC.

Typical Migration

The following *system settings* are migrated in a Typical migration:

- Command Prompt
- Data Sources (ODBC)
- Desktop Settings

    Appearance

    Arrange Icons

    Background

    Desktop Cleanup Wizard

    Folder Options

    Keyboard

    Mouse

- Desktop Settings
  - Regional Settings
  - Screen Saver
  - Send To
  - Sounds
  - Taskbar
  - Time Zone
  - Web Settings
- Dial-Up Networking
- Microsoft IME
- Multilingual UI
- Networking
- Printers
- User Account Settings (XP)

The following *application settings* are migrated in a Typical migration:

- Adobe
  - Acrobat
  - Illustrator
  - InDesign
  - Pagemaker
  - PageMill
  - Photoshop
  - Type Manager Deluxe
- Backup ExecDesktop Pro
- Blackberry Desktop Manager
- Corel
  - Paradox
  - Presentation
  - Quattro Pro
  - WordPerfect

- Eudora Pro
- Exceed
- Executive Software Diskeeper Workstation
- File Maker Pro
- Gold Mine
- HomeSite
- Inoculate IT Anti-Virus Protection
- Internet Explorer
- Lotus
  - 1-2-3
  - Approach
  - Freelance Graphics
  - Notes
  - Organizer
  - WordPro
- Macromedia
  - Director
  - Dreamweaver
  - Fireworks
  - Flash
  - Freehand
- McAfee Virus Scan
- Microsoft
  - Access
  - Excel
  - Exchange
  - FrontPage
  - NetMeeting
  - Office shortcut bar

- Outlook
- Outlook Express
- PowerPoint
- Project
- Word
- MSN
- Netscape Communicator
- Norton
  - Antivirus
  - Ghost
  - Utilities NT
- Novell Networking
- Paint Shop Pro
- Palm Desktop
- PC MACLAN
- pcAnywhere
- Quark Xpress
- Quick View Plus
- Quick Books Pro
- Quicken Deluxe
- Quicken Deluxe 99
- Siebel Sales, Personal Edition
- System Mechanic
- Timbuktu
- Visio
- Windows Messaging
- WinFax Pro
- Winzip

The following *files, folders and file rules (filters)* are migrated in a Typical migration:

- Files included
  - My Documents and sub-folders
- File Rules
- The following extensions are migrated anywhere they exist in the root of local drives and subfolders:
  - *.doc;*.jpg;*.mp3;*.ppt;*.xls

INDEX

Continued

Continued

Continued